CAMBRIDGE LIBRARY COLLECTION

Books of enduring scholarly value

Cambridge

The city of Cambridge received its royal charter in 1201, having already been home to Britons, Romans and Anglo-Saxons for many centuries. Cambridge University was founded soon afterwards and celebrates its octocentenary in 2009. This series explores the history and influence of Cambridge as a centre of science, learning, and discovery, its contributions to national and global politics and culture, and its inevitable controversies and scandals.

Archives of the University of Cambridge

Published in 1962, this account of the University Archives at Cambridge will be of particular importance to those interested in the history of the University. The first part describes the growth of the archives from their beginnings in the thirteenth century and the changes of fortune they have undergone during that time. Part two provides a survey of the archives, placing the main groups in the context of the University. The authors show how the more important classes of archives developed and the places they occupied in the workings of the administration. There are three appendices: a brief summary of the classes mentioned and the dates they cover; a list of muniments of title to landed property; and a bibliography listing published works which have contained or incorporated records from the Archive. There are sixteen illustrations from the Archives themselves.

T0382495

Cambridge University Press has long been a pioneer in the reissuing of out-of-print titles from its own backlist, producing digital reprints of books that are still sought after by scholars and students but could not be reprinted economically using traditional technology. The Cambridge Library Collection extends this activity to a wider range of books which are still of importance to researchers and professionals, either for the source material they contain, or as landmarks in the history of their academic discipline.

Drawing from the world-renowned collections in the Cambridge University Library, and guided by the advice of experts in each subject area, Cambridge University Press is using state-of-the-art scanning machines in its own Printing House to capture the content of each book selected for inclusion. The files are processed to give a consistently clear, crisp image, and the books finished to the high quality standard for which the Press is recognised around the world. The latest print-on-demand technology ensures that the books will remain available indefinitely, and that orders for single or multiple copies can quickly be supplied.

The Cambridge Library Collection will bring back to life books of enduring scholarly value across a wide range of disciplines in the humanities and social sciences and in science and technology.

Archives of the University of Cambridge

An Historical Introduction

HEATHER E. PEEK
CATHERINE P. HALL

CAMBRIDGE
UNIVERSITY PRESS

CAMBRIDGE UNIVERSITY PRESS

Cambridge New York Melbourne Madrid Cape Town Singapore São Paolo Delhi

Published in the United States of America by Cambridge University Press, New York

www.cambridge.org
Information on this title: www.cambridge.org/9781108002370

This edition first published 1962
This digitally printed version 2009

ISBN 978-1-108-00237-0

THE
ARCHIVES OF THE
UNIVERSITY OF
CAMBRIDGE

THE ARCHIVES OF THE UNIVERSITY OF CAMBRIDGE

AN HISTORICAL INTRODUCTION

BY

HEATHER E. PEEK

M.A., F.S.A., F.S.A. Scot.

Keeper of the Archives

AND

CATHERINE P. HALL

M.A.

Sometime Deputy Keeper of the Archives

CAMBRIDGE

AT THE UNIVERSITY PRESS

1962

PUBLISHED BY

THE SYNDICS OF THE CAMBRIDGE UNIVERSITY PRESS

Bentley House, 200 Euston Road, London, N.W. 1
American Branch: 32 East 57th Street, New York 22, N.Y.
West African Office: P.O. Box 33, Ibadan, Nigeria

©

CAMBRIDGE UNIVERSITY PRESS

1962

Printed in Great Britain at the University Press, Cambridge
(Brooke Crutchley, University Printer)

CONTENTS

List of Plates   *page* vi

Preface   vii

PART I

1. The Medieval Archives   I

2. The Registers   6

3. The Custody of the Archives 1550–1960   14

PART II

4. The University and Colleges as Privileged Corporations   24

5. Records of University Administration   27

6. Records of Matriculation and Degrees   30

7. Financial Records of the University   34

8. Endowments of the University   37

9. University Officers and their Records   41

10. Records of the University Courts   48

11. Records of University Jurisdiction in the Town of Cambridge   53

12. The Relations between the Crown and the University   65

13. Other University Institutions and their Records   68

APPENDICES

A. Main Classes of Manuscript Sources in the Archives   72

B. Muniments of Title relating to University Property   74

C. Select Bibliography, 1785–1961   78

Index   87

Index to Muniments of Title in Appendix B   91

LIST OF PLATES

BETWEEN PAGES 64-65

1. Old Proctor's Book, *c.* 1390, fo. 6*a*. Illumination of St Christopher

2. Registrum Librorum, fo. 9*a*. Inventory of the University Archives 1420

3. Transcripts of the privileges of the university presented by Robert Hare, 1587, vol. 1, fo. 17

4. Order of Service for the Commemoration of Benefactors, February 1640/1, pp. 6 and 7

5. Bull of Pope Eugenius IV, 18 September 1433, confirming the exemption of the university from archiepiscopal and episcopal jurisdiction

6. Grant of Arms to the university, 9 June 1573

7. Letters patent for grant of arms of the first five regius professors, 8 November 1590

8. Statutes of 1570, given to the university by Queen Elizabeth I, fos. 3*b* and 4*a*

9. Proctor's Indenture, 1363, accounting for the contents of the Chest

10. Grace Book Δ, fo. 107*b*. Graces for degrees and 'Ordo Senioritatis', 1572

11. Inventory of goods and chattels of Dr Andrew Perne, master of Peterhouse, 1589 (section relating to part of his library)

12. Charter of Edward I (1291/2) confirming the privileges of the university

13. From Robert Hare's transcripts, vol. 1, fo. 276*b*, showing the survey of weights and measures

14. Letters *temp.* Elizabeth I. Original order of Privy Council to Dr Preston, vice-chancellor, enforcing abstention from flesh in Lent, 18 March 1589/90

15. Letters *temp.* Elizabeth I. Burghley to vice-chancellor and heads concerning the establishment of a University Printing Office and appointing Mr Thomas as Printer, 18 March 1582/3

16. A receipted bill relating to the entertainment of Queen Anne in Trinity College, 16 April 1705

PREFACE

It is now nearly fifty years since the Oxford University Press published *A Lecture on the History of the University Archives*, based on one which R. L. Poole, at that time keeper of the archives in the university of Oxford, had given in the Ashmolean Museum. No corresponding account of the archives of Cambridge university has hitherto been published, and this volume is in part an attempt to supply that deficiency. An account of the growth of, and vicissitudes of fortune suffered by, the university muniments in the six centuries of their recorded history, given as a lecture to the Cambridge Antiquarian Society in 1951 by Mrs C. P. Hall, forms the genesis of Part I.

Part II has its origin in a summary guide to the university archives, planned by Miss H. E. Peek, which should set each of the main groups of records within its context of the ancient practice, policies, and traditional ceremonies of the university. The present survey attempts to show the development of the more important classes of archives and their place in the workings of the administration which produced them. It is supplemented by a brief conspectus of the classes mentioned and their covering dates and by a list of muniments of title to landed property, arranged topographically. Finally, a bibliography indicates which records have already been printed *in extenso* or in calendar form, and gives a selection, mainly of modern works, which have drawn upon them for source material.

We wish to thank Professor B. Dickins, Professor M. D. Knowles, Mr W. A. Pantin, Sir Sydney Roberts, and Mr John Saltmarsh for their kindness in reading the whole of the text, and for suggesting various improvements, and Professor Dickins for reading the proofs. To Dr J. P. C. Roach we owe a special debt of gratitude. He has given unsparingly both of his time and of his wide knowledge of the history of the university, and his helpful suggestions have saved us from many pitfalls. We are most grateful to Mr H. C. Whalley-Tooker for reading the chapters on the Records of the University Courts and the Records of University Jurisdiction in the Town of Cambridge; to Dr D. F. McKenzie for help with the chapter on the Press; to Mr C. K. Phillips, deputy treasurer, and Mr A. D. Austin, the treasurer's clerk, for their kindness in reading the chapter on the financial records; to Mr L. C. Hector of the Public Record Office, London, who has given ready assistance over one or two problems connected with the presentation of the illustrations, and to Mr W. G. Rawlings, of the University Library, who has handled the photography with his customary care and skill. We are grateful also to Miss M. E. Raven, assistant to the keeper, for her patience and help with much detailed checking, and to Miss J. M. Lipscombe of the University Registry, and the staff of the General Board for much help with the typing. Two members of our respective families, Mrs Veronica D. Hughes and Mr P. G. Hall, deserve our gratitude for their encouragement and forbearance over the long period of the book's preparation. We wish also to express our gratitude to the publishers for all the trouble and care which they have taken while the book has been going through the press.

H. E. P.

1 December 1961 C. P. H.

PART I

1. THE MEDIEVAL ARCHIVES

The earliest archives of the university, mainly charters of privilege from kings and bishops, were kept with the other valuables belonging to the university in the Common Chest. This practice was general, both for private persons and corporate bodies of all kinds, and indeed the statutes of nearly every medieval college in Oxford and Cambridge, and of the universities themselves, enjoin the safekeeping in chests of the common seal, the plate, the charters, and other important documents. The chests in which these precious articles were deposited were made of stout oak planks from two to three inches thick, bound with iron bands and secured by locks and padlocks of different wards, so as to require the presence of several officials at the same time to open them. One such chest, dating from the later Middle Ages, is still in the registrary's room and has five different locks. The keys were held by the chancellor (or vice-chancellor), the two proctors, and two non-regent masters chosen for this purpose. Regulations for the election of these masters, for opening the Common Chest and for keeping an account of the contents were laid down in the ancient 'Statuta'.[1] The annual audit was held 'within 8 days of the feast of St Dionysius' (9 October) and at this an indenture was drawn up between the outgoing and incoming officers, enumerating the contents of the Chest. The outgoing proctors kept one half as their acquittance and the other was deposited in the Chest. All the earlier indentures have perished except that of 1363, which survives by a fortunate piece of misplacing.[2] In that year the Chest contained: money to the value of £32. 12s. 3¾d. with notes of other small sums owed, an alabaster cup placed as a pledge, four books of canon law and one of the 'Sentences',[3] a set of Mass vestments with a cope, a white vestment, and a dozen silk cloths; finally the charters, which begin with the item '33 royal

---

[1] 'Statuta Antiqua'. Printed in *Documents relating to the University and Colleges of Cambridge* (London, 1852), vol. I, pp. 295 ff., particularly nos. 58, 181–3 and 188.

[2] Transcribed and printed in Introduction to Grace Book Γ, p. x (plate 9).

[3] 'Sententiarum libri quatuor', by the 12th century Peter Lombard.

charters and 2 letters patent'. Some of these charters remain to this day but many have disappeared.

The university owned from the fourteenth century, in addition to the Common Chest, certain 'charitable' chests, which had been endowed by benefactors for making loans to poor students or for providing chaplains and chantries for the keeping of obits. One of these, the Neel Chest, incorporates in its foundation deed (1344) an elaborate set of statutes modelled on the arrangements for the keeping of the Common Chest;[1] and there is reason for thinking that the Neel Chest and perhaps others were kept with the Common Chest in the university treasury. Neither the university of Oxford nor that of Cambridge possessed at this time stone buildings suitable for the safe keeping of treasure, and both made use of the university church. At Oxford the treasury from about 1320 was in the Old Congregation House of St Mary the Virgin,[2] and at Cambridge in the tower of Great St Mary's.

It was to Great St Mary's that the rioters came in June 1381, during the disturbances in which the university archives played a prominent but unfortunate part. The story of the bonfire on Market Hill, in which so many of the early muniments perished at the hands of the townsmen, is familiar to us from the picturesque account in Cooper's *Annals*.[3] Perhaps less well known is the following extract from a memorandum in the Parliament Rolls. Here the place in which the Common Chest was kept is explicitly referred to as 'Le Tresorie'.[4]

Fait a remembrer qe grantz pleintes et clamour estoient faitz en ceste Parlement des Mair Baillifs et la Comminaltee de la Ville de Cantebrugge, de ce qe en temps del rumour et levee de malurez gentz ils avec plusours autres malfaisours de lours assent et covine en oultrageouses multitudes qi estoient venuz a lour envoie a la dite Ville de Cantebrugge lesqueux entre autres lours malfaites debriserent le Tresorie de l'Universitee illoeqes et les Privileges et Chartres des Rois, Bulles del Pape, et autres Munimentz del dite Universite arderent...

Et adonqes le dit Esmon nadgairs Mair illoeqes present respondist et dist...Q'il ne fust unqes assentant aidant ne conseillant au dit malfait...ne rienz unqes y fist ne deist qe y purroit eschere en damage ou deshoneur de la dite Universitee sinoun soulement par cohercion et oultrageous compulsion dautres.[5]

[1] Document no. 35 (Luard's list). Printed and described by J. W. Clark, *Camb. Ant. Soc. Proc.* vol. XI (O.S.), no. XLV, pp. 82–95.
[2] Reginald L. Poole, *A Lecture on the History of the University Archives* [Oxford], (Oxford, 1912), p. 7.
[3] C. H. Cooper, *Annals of Cambridge* (Cambridge, 1842), vol. I, pp. 120–1 (for 1381).
[4] *Rot. Parl.* 5° Ric. II, pt. I, m. 9. Printed in 'Rotuli Parliamentorum', vol. III, pp. 106–7.
[5] 'It is to be remembered that great complaints and clamour were made in this Parliament against the Mayor, Bailiffs and Commonalty of the Town of Cambridge, for the fact that, in a time of unrest and uprising of

Although this catastrophe undoubtedly sadly depleted the charters of the university, a certain number escaped the fury of the rioters. About forty such for the period 1266–1381 are recorded in fifteenth-century lists. Further royal charters, confirming privileges and conferring new ones, were soon added to this nucleus, so that their number was almost doubled in the next four decades. With this recovery, the university found a new and safer place for its treasury.

In the last decade of the fourteenth century Sir William Thorpe, brother of the lord chancellor, and the Lady Grace, his wife, devoted themselves to the building of the new Divinity Schools, which the university had begun to erect on land received from the bequest of Nigel de Thornton. Two earlier attempts had been made to finish the work in 1359 and 1365 but had been brought to a standstill from lack of funds. Sir William Thorpe now revived the project, and in 1400 brought the building to its completion, largely as it stands today. Below was the Divinity School, above a chapel, generally called the 'New Chapel', which could be used both for ordinary assemblies of the university and for the commemoration of benefactors. In return for their munificence, Sir William and Lady Grace were to benefit from this latter use. In 1398 the university under its chancellor, Eudo de la Zouche, covenanted to pray for them while they lived, and celebrate their exequies after their death. Further, every graduate on his admission was required to say a 'De profundis' for them. This covenant was embodied in the statutes,[1] and referring to it Archbishop Parker says: 'For which Convention, the Executors of William Thorpe went forward with the Divinity Scholes,... making from the ground the Porch, with the foundation, and the volte as it standeth at this day, where the University Hutch is.'[2]

seditious people, they, with many other like-minded evildoers of whom they approved, who had come in enormous multitudes at their summons to the said Town of Cambridge, among their other misdeeds broke open the Treasury of the University there, and burned the Privileges and Charters of the Kings, the Bulls of the Pope and other Muniments of the said University'. . .

'Whereupon the said Edmund, lately Mayor, being there present, replied and said, . . . that he had never agreed to, helped nor advised the said misdeed . . . and that he neither did nor said anything there which might have resulted in damage or dishonour to the said University, save solely on the coercion and violent compulsion by others.'

[1] 'Statuta Antiqua' no. 184. Printed in *Documents relating...*, vol. I, p. 411.

[2] MS. 118, no. 6, in Corpus Christi College (C.C.C.). Printed in H. P. Stokes, *The Chaplains and the Chapel of the University of Cambridge*, Cambridge Antiquarian Society 8° publication, no. XLI, pp. 21, 49 and 51. See also Robert Willis and John Willis Clark, *The Architectural History of the University of Cambridge* (Cambridge, 1886), vol. III, p. 11.

This 'little volte' was the second home of the University Chest. It seems to have been a smaller chapel or vestry built over the staircase leading up to the New Chapel (now generally known as the Regent House). The doorway by which it was entered from the New Chapel is still visible, but it and the staircase were removed during alterations to the Old Schools in the seventeenth century. Of its appearance, therefore, little is known except that it had a window, as appears from an entry in the Proctors' Accounts of 1518: 'pro vitriacione cujusdam fenestre in parvo sacello in scholis...vj^d'. The keys of the room, according to Parker, were to be in the custody of the vice-chancellor.

At what date this room became the university treasury is not known. It must have been before 1458, when an entry in Grace Book A refers to the room as 'capella ciste communis', though its more usual title at this time was 'parva capella' (as in Statute 63 which speaks of 'nova capella et parva capella eidem annexa'). By 1513 the room was 'Ye Universyte Chapell vestrary' and later simply 'the Vestry'. There seems no reason why the Chest should not have been moved across from Great St Mary's soon after the completion of the new building, as the presence of a permanent 'Keeper of the Schools' there made it safer than the church had been. It seems likely that the Chest was in the vestry by 1420, when a certain Master William Rysley compiled a very detailed inventory of the contents of the Chest; for on the last leaf of this inventory is the 'Registrum vestimentorum et aliorum ornamentorum ad novam capellam universitatis Cantebrigie pertinencium'. The register of vestments is not in Rysley's hand but in one similar to that of the writer of the Library List of 1424 which follows it in the volume as made up.[1] All these lists were subsequently bound up into the 'Registrum Librorum, Scriptorum, aliorumque bonorum Universitatis', compiled by the proctors in 1473 and preserved in this form in the university archives.

Rysley's inventory of 1420 deserves more detailed description, since, in listing the contents of the Chest, it incidentally becomes the first catalogue of the archives. It is written on four parchment sheets of indifferent quality, with holes and snags, folded to form a gathering of eight leaves. Of these, the first five are ruled for the inventory proper, the fifth is mutilated, the sixth and seventh left blank, except for the register of vestments on fo. 7b, and the eighth is cut away. The inventory is headed: 'Inventarium bonorum mobilium ad cistam com-

[1] Transcribed by H. Bradshaw, *Camb. Ant. Soc. Proc.* vol. II (O.S.), no. XXII, pp. 242–57.

munem universitatis Cantebrigg pertinencium sub anno domini millesimo cccc° xx° et Henrici quinti viii per magistrum Willelmum Rysley compilatum.'[1]

First the valuables are listed: the university seal of silver, and three purses; the 'common purse', a purse of Master Robert Tey containing £6, and a purse of rents from the university lands and the new School of Civil Law. Then come the muniments, roughly classified and kept in smaller bags or boxes marked A–N, and within these boxes the documents bear individual letters, a, b, c. Boxes A–D are entitled 'Indulta Regum' and contain charters from Henry III to Henry V, seventy in all; box F has sixteen 'Indulta et Epistole summorum Pontificum'; and box G, 'Composiciones et concordie Universitatem tangentes cum aliis', twenty-three in number. Boxes H and I are devoted to muniments connected with the early benefactors, Nigel de Thornton and Roger Heedon. Rysley did not complete the inventory of the last five boxes. For box K he entered eight indentures and leases of property, and for box L two commissions. Box M is headed, 'Obligaciones et acquietancie' but nothing is listed. Box N has six 'Bille cum aliis memorabilibus'. Below this is a pointing finger in the margin and two notes: 'Item memorandum quod Johannes Aylmer contulit universitati unum ciphum argenteum cum coopertorio cum iii angulis in pede ponderis i lb vii unc' et v peny weght et hoc ad usum cancellarii qui pro tempore fuerit. Magister Willelmus Rysley istud inventarium compilavit et manu propria scripcit. Anno domini m^{mo} cccc^{mo} xx°.'

Rysley's inventory at once became the standard list by which the muniments were checked. From at least 1431, the writers of the Proctors' Indentures, accounting for the contents of the Chest, avoided the necessity of enumerating the earlier charters by the convenient formula 'Item munimenta que continentur in registro compilato per M. Rysley usque ad M. literam...', and then made any additions or corrections.

From these indentures, and indeed from the earlier indentures of 1363, we find that the University Chest contained, besides valuables and muniments, notes of debts, and also pledges for loans or debts, generally termed 'cautions'. During the fifteenth century, the increasing bulk of the archives and the increased numbers of pledges made it necessary to provide a separate chest for these cautions. A statute was accordingly made in June 1456 authorising the provision of a chest

[1] Registrum Librorum, fo. 9a (plate 2).

of three keys, to be kept by the vice-chancellor and the proctors, for the safe keeping of the cautions, 'since many of them are not in money but consist of books or other things'.[1] At a later date, some of the archives themselves had to be moved from the Common Chest to another, generally called the 'Chest of Evidences'. In 1487 the Grace Book has an entry, 'Item pro uno [sic] clavi ad cistam evidenciarum . . . viijᵈ'.[2] Both these chests were kept with the Common Chest in the vestry.

Although the archives were being added to in every decade, Rysley's inventory remained the only catalogue for two centuries after it was written. Until about 1500, it was corrected and kept up to date by various writers. The latest and most thorough of these revisions is made in a hand identical with that of the Senior Proctor's Account of 1494–5 in Grace Book B. The senior proctor in that year was John Fisher and the hand is believed to be his. Fisher, if indeed it was he, evidently made a very careful check of the whole of the contents of the Chest and against several sections wrote 'non reperiuntur' in the margin. As well as adding new documents he prefaced the inventory with a short instruction on how to find individual documents: 'Quisquis ad cistam hanc accedis quippiam quesiturus perlege primum istum indicem in quo ubi reperieris rem tuam; deprehendes duplicem litteram alteram capitalem alteram minorem. Capitalis littera docebit pixidem, minor vero locum pixidis iuxta litterarum ordinem.'

Whether much use was made of the revised catalogue is doubtful, for after this all additional entries cease. In the new century were to come administrative and other changes which would rapidly render obsolete many of the medieval muniments of the university.

2. THE REGISTERS

The sixteenth century opened in the universities with a burst of administrative activity and of reform in the keeping of administrative records. A second period of expansion took place between 1540 and 1550. As a result, there arose the third great group of university documents (after the charters and deeds of property), the 'registers', and with them a new officer whose duty it was to keep them, the registrary. Similar developments took place in Oxford, some slightly before,

[1] 'Statuta Antiqua' no. 59. Printed in Documents relating . . . , vol. I, p. 343.
[2] Grace Book A, p. 219 (fo. 149b).

some slightly after, their Cambridge equivalents, so that in this matter at least Cambridge was not merely following the lead of the senior university.

At Cambridge, the year 1501 is the starting-point for the changes, and perhaps it is not a coincidence that John Fisher became vice-chancellor in that year. Certainly he was a skilled administrator and had personal knowledge of the keeping of university records from his proctorship. Up to this time there had been only one series of registers, the 'Registra Procuratorum', kept by each pair of proctors during their year of office. Although primarily financial records, these 'Registra' had contained a considerable amount of other matter, Graces for degrees, the 'Ordo Senioritatis', and acts of the senate. In 1501 it was decided that the 'Registra' should be confined to matters financial, while the Graces of the senate, the Ordo and similar acts should be entered in a new book. Thus was inaugurated the series of Grace Books proper.[1] Another reform of this year concerned the keeping of a Register of Wills proved in the chancellor's court, and the first extant book of copies of wills begins in 1501.

The question then arises, who kept these registers? The curious thing is that five years elapse before their keeping is made the subject of university legislation. In Grace Book Γ there is an entry, for the year 1506, 'Item conceditur magistro Robarto Hobbys bedello artium ut sit regestrarius universitatis', together with a Grace that on account of his office he shall be excused attendance at exequies and masses 'salva regencia sua'.[2] Hobbys had been a fellow of King's College, held the degree of M.A. and had been made bedell of arts the previous year. As the entries in the Grace Book are in his hand from the year of his bedellship, it may be that from its inception the Grace Book had been kept by one of the esquire bedells. The hands of the earlier entries do not change annually as in the Proctors' Register. More cannot be proved, as we have no examples of the hands of earlier bedells with which to make comparisons. What is certain is that the office of registrary continued to be given to one of the bedells until the seventeenth century.

Little more is known of Hobbys' activities as registrary. In 1507 he was allowed by Grace to remain covered in congregations 'propter egritudinem quam habet in capite',[3] but it cannot have been a serious complaint, for while he resigned the office of bedell in 1529, he retained that of registrary until 1542–3, when he made

---

[1] See chapter 5, on Grace Books.   [2] *Grace Book* Γ, p. 51 (fo. 31*a*).   [3] *Ibid.* p. 63 (fo. 37*a*).

his last entry in the Grace Book, recording his retirement and the appointment of John Mere.[1]

John Mere, like his predecessor, was an M.A. and had been a fellow of King's. He had been bedell of divinity since July 1530. He resigned the bedellship in 1557 but remained registrary until his death in 1558. As registrary, Mere has left us evidence of his care and diligence in office, and the entries in the new Grace Book[2] he began are regularly made in a neat, splayed hand. In his hand also is a fragment of the 'Acta Curiae' for the year 1552, showing that it now fell to the registrary to keep the ordinary judicial records,[3] as well as the Books of Wills. From the statute of 1544,[4] which initiated the system of university matriculation, the Registrary kept the Matriculation Register. All this was in addition to his work as esquire bedell, work which took him to London at times on university business, for we have two bills of his expenses in the years 1548 and 1554, the latter signed. He was the author of three diaries, one of which (that for the year 1533–4) is written on blank pages of Grace Book A.[5] It is significant that he had custody of this register while he was a bedell only.

While he was in office, Mere evidently compiled notes relating to university privileges and procedure, for, according to his will, his executors were to 'gyve to the Registers offyce of thuniversytie as wel those bokes that I bought as those that I have made myself concernying that offyce, so that they remayn perpetually to the offyce'. Corpus Christi College has preserved the record of this transaction, a bill between Mere's executors and his successor in office, which enumerates the registers in detail. Most of them can be identified with existing volumes.[6]

The registers were not Mere's only gift to the university. The house he bequeathed became for many years the home of the Lady Margaret Professor, and its title deeds remain in the university archives (see also chap. 8). As well as this benefaction of 'my holl house wherein I do nowe dwel', Mere left 'the reversion and

---

[1] Grace Book Γ, p. 369 (fo. 177b).
[2] Grace Book Δ.   [3] See chapter 11, on 'University Jurisdiction'.
[4] Statute of 11 May 1544. Statuta Academiae Cantabrigiensis (ed. of 1785), p. 122.
[5] Grace Book A, pp. 221–30 (fos. 52a–55b). The other diaries are edited by John Lamb, A Collection of Letters, Statutes and other Documents from the Manuscript Library of Corpus Christi College (London, 1838), pp. 184–236.
[6] MS. 106, no. 346 in Corpus Christi College. Transcripts in Cambridge University Registry guard-book (henceforward referred to as C.U.R.) 20.1 (Registrary), no. 3 (*2) and documents relating to the probate of Mere's will in 'Exhibita' files. See Appendix A for a description of the guard-books.

yeres remayngynge in my lease of the house and gardens over the waye agaynst my sayd house provided that my father for the tyme of his dweling in Cambridge may have a competent chamber in the house aforsayd with a bed fornyshed in the same for his use...also I gyve to Mr Vice-Chancellor a gold ryng to the value of xs.'. In 1559 Mere's executors founded the sermon still observed as 'Mere's Commemoration' and he is, of course, remembered among the university benefactors. He was buried, according to his own wish, 'in the churchyeard of St Bene't's next to my late wyfe deceased whose sowle God pardon'. The tomb-stone can still be identified, but the present inscription is of a later date.

The work so well begun by Hobbys and Mere was continued by the third registrary, Matthew Stokys, bedell of divinity and notary public. Stokys was elected in 1558 at a critical time for the university when religious and social changes had wrought havoc with ancient practice and administration. He saw the university jurisdiction, which had been principally ecclesiastical, become more secular, and the promulgation of the new statutes of 1570, which were to form the basis of university administration for the next three centuries. Fortunately, Stokys seems to have been a model registrary, preserving the old and adapting himself to the new. Fuller says of him:

A register [he was] indeed, both by his place and painful performance therein; for he (as the Poets fain of Janus with two faces) saw two worlds, that before and after the Reformation; in which juncture of time, so great the confusion and embezzling of records, that, had not Master Stokes been the more careful, I believe, that though Cambridge would not be so oblivious as Massala Corvinus, who forgot his own name, yet would she have forgotten the names of all her ancient officers.[1]

The book which he compiled on the ancient officers and practices of the university is still in the university archives and one of its greatest treasures.[2] Stokys was also responsible for the re-designing of the common seal of the university in its present form, and for a curious diagram depicting the duties of the clerks of the market. This and his coat of arms still hang in the registry.

The new statutes of 1570, and the industry of the registrary, meant a great increase in the numbers of the university records. The court records alone were beginning to assume unwieldy proportions. Probably spurred on by the energetic

---

[1] Thomas Fuller, *The History of the Worthies of England* (Nuttall's edn., 3 vols., London, 1840), vol. I, p. 206.

[2] 'Stokys' Book', fos. 89b–113a. Transcripts of portions of Stokys' Book in Appendix A of G. Peacock, *Observations on the Statutes of the University of Cambridge* (London and Cambridge, 1841).

registrary, the university provided the first permanent home of the registry office. In 1571–2 the east side of the Schools' quadrangle, which had originally contained two small schools, was converted for the use of the vice-chancellor's court and the registrary. The account runs:

Item to Matthewe Stokys Bedell, to glase and to make thowse on the sowthe syde of the scoole gatys a consistorie for the Vice-Chauncelours and an office for ye Regester to kepe the bokes and recordys of thuniversitie in...ix[li] ix[s].[1]

The use of the term 'register' for the office was general at this date and persisted at least to the mid-seventeenth century, when the civil 'registers' for births and deaths were created under the Commonwealth. With regard to the duties of the 'university register', inscribed in the fly-leaf of Grace Book B is a short poem:

> Who deue wilbe a Register
> shulde holde his pen in truthe entyere
> Ensearch he ought recordes of olde
> the dowte to trye; the right to holde
> The lawes to know he must co[n]tende
> Olde customys eke: he shulde expende
> No paynes to wright he maye refuse
> His offyce ellys: he dothe abuse.

In the first half of the seventeenth century, the registry, the 'State Paper Office' of the university, continued to expand. Indeed, under the energetic and respected James Tabor, registrary from 1600 to 1645, the registry office may be said to have been in its hey-day, and the registrary himself an increasingly important person in the affairs of the university.

With Tabor, the office of registrary was finally dissociated from that of esquire bedell. Some of the earlier registraries had perhaps anticipated this development by retaining office after they had resigned their bedellship (presumably because the duties of the latter office were more onerous to the aged or infirm), but, until Tabor's appointment, every new registrary had been one of the esquire bedells. Tabor himself, however, M.A. of Corpus Christi College and a notary public, held no other position than that of Clerk to the Commissioners of Sewers. He kept the records assiduously, particularly the court records, and we have more miscellaneous bills, receipts, warrants, and memoranda preserved from his period

---

[1] University Audit Book, 1545–1659, fo. 123 b. Willis and Clark, *Architectural History*, vol. III, p. 22.

of office than from any other prior to the nineteenth century. Tabor (according to a note made by an unidentified writer in one of the registrary's volumes) was considered by his contemporaries to be 'a man of worth and skill in his business'. His opinion was frequently sought, for we have memoranda by him on such matters as 'whether the Proctor should be the Vice-Chancellors Assessor', 'the University right of Printing', and the 'Lordshipp of the Soyle'. In the activity which followed Archbishop Laud's proposal to visit as metropolitan,[1] Tabor was the leading spirit, and earned the congratulations of the lord high steward, the Earl of Manchester. 'I do much commend the care and diligence I see your register useth', he wrote, 'in preserving and being so ready in these things that concern your university rights and privileges.' In fact the only complaint that can be brought against the excellent Tabor is the difficulty of his handwriting.

Tabor's predecessor in office, Thomas Smith, had not been so exemplary. His Grace Book contains a bare list of those who proceeded to degrees, very cramped together. The court records have many gaps in the neat 'Acta Curiae' registers and for his term of office the Matriculation Register shows a complete blank. Under registrary Smith, many of the records which should have been in the register office were allowed to go out of custody, and a large number of these were left in the study of Dr Preston of Trinity Hall, who had been vice-chancellor when Smith came into office. The documents were found by Dr Jegon and delivered to registrary Tabor, who listed them in his usual careful manner, and noted at the foot 'received theise particulars by the handes of Dr Jegon this 23 of Marche 1601'.[2] The documents thus transferred included not only letters and memoranda but also the Proctors' Leet Rolls and the royal charter of 31 Elizabeth. In fairness to Smith it should perhaps be added that the proper collection of the university papers in the registry office must have been a formidable task. At that time, the business papers of any office-holder were considered his private property, and even the central State Paper Office failed to receive the papers of all the secretaries of state. How much more difficult the situation in the university with its frequently changing officers, and in how many studies in how many different colleges might not valuable documents be lying? In fact, with the awakening of 'archive-consciousness' in the nineteenth century, quite a number

---

[1] J. B. Mullinger, *The University of Cambridge* (Cambridge, 1873–1911), vol. III, pp. 124–6, 131–4.
[2] C.U.R. 20. 1 (Registrary), no. 6 (1).

of valuable books and registers were rediscovered in the colleges and returned to the registry.[1]

With regard to the activities of registrary Tabor, we find that the work of the registrary had increased greatly since the time of John Mere. As an additional check on the various registers, it had become the practice under Matthew Stokys to file the original documents from which they were compiled. Thus, with the Grace Books went the series of Original Graces, 'Ordo Senioritatis' on separate slips, and the 'Supplicats' for degrees sent in by the college praelectors. With the Matriculation Register went the Praelectors' Lists. As well as the neat 'Acta Curiae' series, there were files of 'Exhibita' and odd notebooks and papers with depositions, rough notes and so on. From the year 1613, a new task was added to the registrary's labours, the series of Subscriptions to the oaths, required by royal command, first of doctors and then of all recipients of degrees.[2] This extra task proved such a burden that, in 1623, Tabor sent a petition to the crown that he might at least have a fee for his pains.[3] The king referred the matter to the vice-chancellor and heads, who thereupon passed decrees providing for a fee of sixpence per head, and for a more orderly method of taking the subscriptions, 'because heretofore there hath been great disorder at the times of subscription by the unruly crouding and striving of those which were to subscribe whereby the register attending that service hath been discouraged and wronged'.

After the registers, the registrary had in his custody various volumes of memoranda and collectanea which from the time of Mere had been compiled as the reference books of the office. To these Tabor added, in 1629, one of his own, generally known as 'Tabor's Book', containing 'A Breif of all the chief matters contained in Mr Hares Fower bookes'[4] and sundry other notes. At the back of this volume is a list which records some of the other contents of the registry office, the endless loose papers and notebooks relating to the varied business of the university—elections to offices, awarding of prizes, licensing of preachers and surgeons, licensing of vintners and victuallers, the assize of bread and ale, the regulations of fairs and markets, the sewers, the poor rate—to mention but a few. The list is entitled 'A Note of what is conteyned in the Severall Boxes'[5] and is evidently

[1] 'Markaunt's Book' was restored to custody by Robert Hare, M. Wren, and again by T. Baker. The 'Old Vice-Chancellor's Book' and Mere's 'Liber Rerum Memorabilium' were recovered in the nineteenth century.

[2] Subscription Register, no. 1, fos. 2 and 3.

[3] C.U.R. 20.1 (Registry), no. 6 (8).   [4] Hare's transcripts.   [5] 'Tabor's Book', fo. 732.

written by a clerk and corrected in Tabor's own hand. Its date must be shortly after 1630 as it mentions 'Dr Wren's yere' (1628–9) and Dr Butts, who was vice-chancellor at the time of the plague outbreak of 1630. Even if the list is not quite complete, it gives us a fairly comprehensive picture of the multitude of matters with which the register office had to be concerned.

The venerable and respected registrary Tabor died in July 1645, having held office from the reign of Elizabeth almost to the eve of the Commonwealth. He was succeeded by Matthew Whinn, who had risen from very humble beginnings to occupy this honourable position in the university. The son of a local tailor, he entered St John's College as a sizar at the age of eighteen. After graduating he became a notary public in 1643 and two years afterwards was elected registrary while still in his early thirties. He remained registrary for nearly forty years, un-affected by the victory of the parliament or the return of the king. In 1669 he was made university printer and continued to hold both his offices until his death in 1683.

On accession to the office of 'register' his first act seems to have been to complain that his profits were inadequate, and in the following year a Grace of the senate raised the registrary's fees on each degree to a shilling.[1] In return for this con-cession, however, the university demanded an efficient discharge of duties on the part of the registrary. In April 1647 an elaborate Grace passed the senate which may be roughly summarised thus:[2]

That since the acts of the university, records of letters and gifts, causes at law, etc., ought to be preserved for use and reference, and since the registrary's stipend was recently raised so that he ought to be more diligent in the discharge of his duties; it is ordered that a record book for the use of the senate be prepared by the registrary immediately, containing all the acts, etc., of the senate, entered under their proper titles and with a rational index. Moreover the acta of each term shall be entered within ten days of the end of term in their appropriate places. The registrary shall be present with this record at all congregations and at the audit of the accounts. Penalties are decreed for negligence on the part of the registrary, who is to be removed from office on the fifth offence. This grace is to be added to the statutes and inscribed in the front of the said record book.

[1] C.U.R. 20.1 (Registrary), no. 7 (3).
[2] Grace Book H, fo. 27, and printed in *Statuta Academiae Cantabrigiensis* (1785), p. 390.

In spite of this activity on the part of the senate and the severity of the penalties for negligence, Whinn has not left behind him the reputation of being a particularly good registrary. The odd letters and notes of his in the university archives today are not the work of a methodical man but untidily scribbled on torn scraps of paper. His minute book, a small paper notebook of some two dozen pages, is largely blank and the memoranda it does contain of the briefest. More damning is the note by an anonymous writer in the volume now known as 'Tabor's Book'. Whinn, it seems, found this book in the registry, made a few additions of his own, and then presented it to the university, inscribed as his own gift. But a slightly later hand has added the comment: 'This collection is chiefly owing to Tabor ye Register to wch Whinn added a few things. So y^t it ought to be call'd Tabor's Book, and not Whinns. Tabor was a man of worth and skill in his business. Whinn a man so mean y^t he could neither make, nor so much as faithfully transcribe true Latin; wch is as notorious as y^t he was Register.'[1]

3. THE CUSTODY OF THE ARCHIVES
1550-1960

While the registrary was concerned with producing and keeping the records of university administration and jurisdiction, his authority did not originally extend to the custody of the older muniments of the university. In fact a sharp distinction was drawn between the 'registers', books and papers which were housed in the register office and consistory, and 'muniments' or 'archives'. These latter were still considered to be part of the university treasure to be kept by the vice-chancellor and proctors, in whose hands all financial control was vested. These archives therefore remained in the vestry, seldom seeing the light of day between one audit and the next. It was small wonder that, in the course of half a century of neglect, a general ignorance of their contents prevailed.

In the spring of 1552–3 the university was engaged in one of its frequent quarrels with the town, and it occurred to someone that an investigation of the ancient muniments of the university might reveal privileges which would enable the

---

[1] 'Tabor's Book', fly-leaf.

university to score in such disputes. Accordingly a Grace was passed by the senate,[1] deploring the neglected state of the documents, and appointing a commission to examine them, noting especially anything which concerned the liberties and laws of the university, and to inscribe them in a book. The Grace concludes with a request that the ancient statutes in the Proctor's Books may be similarly examined and revised. This Grace incidentally marks the first of various sporadic attempts to codify the privileges and statutes of the university, a task not really performed until 1785. We hear no more of this commission, but in view of the unsettled times which followed the accession of Queen Mary perhaps this is not surprising.

If the archives themselves remained untouched, the early years of Queen Elizabeth's reign saw sweeping changes in the vestry in which they were housed. An 'Inventory of goods perteyning to the Universitie remayning in the Vestry' (1562) gives: 'Item the common chiste for thuniversitie', 'Item a chiste with evydences and charters',[2] among an impressive collection of vestments and chapel furnishings.

Two years later order was given by Grace for the sale of the 'superstitious monumentes, whereof by publicke order takyn there is presently no use, being now in the vestrie';[3] and a small paper of 1565, recently discovered in the university archives, gives details of the valuation of the vestments, etc. and their purchasers. An inventory of 1585, revealing a much denuded vestry, still retains 'Two Chists bound with iron'.[4] The muniments remained but as relics of a bygone age. The great Elizabethan code of statutes of 1570, with other royal charters cited in the Act for the Incorporation of the Universities of 1571, so largely superseded the old arrangements that the ancient archives were no longer useful for current reference and seldom needed for defence of privilege.

If the university as a whole was more concerned with adjusting itself to the new age than with preserving the relics of the old, some there were to whom the old ways were dear, and among them the indefatigable antiquary, Robert Hare,

---

[1] *Grace Book Δ*, p. 89 (fo. 36a).
[2] C.U.R. 78 (University Miscellanea), no. 15. Printed by H. P. Stokes in *The Chaplains and the Chapel of the University of Cambridge*, p. 65.
[3] *Grace Book Δ*, p. 191 (fo. 84a).
[4] Inventory of 1585, printed by H. P. Stokes in *The Chaplains and the Chapel of the University of Cambridge*, p. 69.

clerk of the pells to Queen Elizabeth I. Hare was incidentally a great personal friend and ultimately executor of that Dr Mowse who had been a member of the commission of 1552. Among his many activities he compiled two great collections of transcripts relating to the privileges of the universities of Oxford and Cambridge, basing them chiefly on documents in the central records, to which he had access in his office, but also in part on the documents of the universities themselves. Hare caused a handsome presentation copy of his Cambridge transcripts to be made on vellum, in two volumes, and presented it to the university in 1587.[1] At his death he bequeathed his original copies to the university also, so that the vice-chancellor had the use of one set and the registrary of the other. Hare's transcripts have since proved invaluable, for they preserve the text of documents since lost or decayed and have been used more frequently than any other volumes in the university archives. It is to be feared, however, that the very excellence of Hare's work defeated its own ends, for with readable indexed transcripts in the register office, who would care to ferret among the disordered and crabbed originals?

The condition of the archives did not concern the senate again until 1620, in which year it was discovered that some of the muniments had been removed from the Chest and could not be produced when needed. This was serious, for no transcript could be substituted for an original document in the sight of a court of law. A commission was therefore appointed by Grace on 7 July of that year, with authority to sort and check the archives and, if possible, to recover stray documents.[2] All were to be replaced in safe custody and provision was to be made to prevent any future removal of documents from the chapel. For some unstated reason, however, this 'review of ye monuments' (as the Grace Book calls it) never took place. By Grace of 15 December 1621, a second commission was appointed to examine the archives, arrange them in order, and see that they were in safe custody, so that they might be 'of public use'.[3] The sort of 'public use' in the minds of the promoters of the Grace is shown by the next entry in the book, the appointment of a further commission to inquire into the true extent and value of all properties and rights of the university in the town of Cambridge and elsewhere.

The Archive Commission was to consist of the vice-chancellor, Dr Jerome Beale of Pembroke College, two other heads, Dr Gostlin of Caius and Dr Paske of Clare, the two proctors, the registrary and two masters of arts. Each of these

[1] Plate 3.   [2] Grace Book E, fo. 311.   [3] Grace Book Z, fo. 37.

last, by a strange coincidence, was destined to become master of Peterhouse and bishop, for they were Matthew Wren and John Cosin. Our chief concern is, however, with the former. Wren had been a fellow of Pembroke since 1605, and in 1616 was made president (that is, vice-master). It was he who began the proper college register of admissions; he was also the first to write a proper catalogue of the college statutes and to put the manuscripts in the college library in order.[1] It was doubtless his experience in such matters which caused him to be chosen to sit on the commission and to become its scribe.

The catalogue which Matthew Wren compiled as a result of his survey of the muniments is written in his own neat, italic hand on the blank leaves of the back of the Proctors' Inventory of 1473.[2] It is headed 'Scripta et Munimenta reperta in Archivis Academiae. A. 1622'. Then comes a brief explanation of his system of identification, which superficially is similar to Rysley's but, whereas Rysley's boxes contain documents of a kind in chronological order, Wren's location marks were obviously put on the documents as he found them and consequently have very little method or order. It is, therefore, not surprising to find Wren's attempts at an ordered catalogue less successful than Rysley's. Like his predecessor Wren begins with a section entitled 'Regum Cartae Scriptaque alia' and intends the entries to be in chronological order, but several of the charters he misplaces or fails to assign to their proper monarch. In all ninety-one charters are entered. The second section, 'Pontificum et Episcoporum', is more orderly but is a much smaller section of only twenty documents. At section three, 'Universitatis Fundi', Wren departs from the earlier arrangement for obvious reasons. In 1420 university property had hardly existed beyond the site of the Old Schools and its accompanying 'Lands'; but by 1622 there are five main properties; 'The Crow' on Senate House Hill, Mere's House, Burwell Vicarage and Rectory, and Parker's gift, Regent Walk. The lectureships mentioned in section four (the Lady Margaret Lectureship and Preachership and Rede Lectureship) were not endowed until the sixteenth century. In the last section, 'Acta Aliaque Scripta ipsius Universitatis', all the remaining ancient documents are gathered, making an enormous 'miscellanea' of fifty-seven pieces. The arrangement is chronological, with the exception of the last eight entries, for which Wren could find no date.

---

[1] Aubrey Leonard Attwater, *Pembroke College, Cambridge: A Short History* (Cambridge, 1936), pp. 65–6.
[2] 'Registrum Librorum', which contains Rysley's catalogue.

As most of these have a date appearing somewhere in the text, it seems that Wren relied on the docketing of others rather than on scrutiny of the texts. In all, Wren's catalogue covers 235 documents (a few of these are duplicates), the majority of which can be identified both with documents mentioned by Rysley (if prior to 1420) and with documents still retained in the university archives.

Although Wren's catalogue includes almost all the important charters of which we have evidence up to the reign of Edward VI, here it stops abruptly. With the exception of the great Elizabethan statutes of 1570, the charters of Elizabeth and James I are not mentioned, although there are in fact several handsome and important ones in the university collection from that period. A few of the more recent deeds of property are, however, included. Space and convenience probably dictated this further stage in the isolation of the ancient muniments from the records of current university administration. The chests in the vestry were already overfull with largely obsolete documents, and could not accommodate the massive royal charters of the Elizabethan and later periods. In any case, it would be more convenient to have them in the register office where they could be consulted.

It is doubtful whether the ancient archives as listed by Wren were in fact used at all in subsequent years. Two possible occasions may be adduced, before the troubles of the Civil War cause us to lose sight of the archives altogether. First, at the time of Laud's proposed visitation in 1635, precedents were eagerly sought to prove the university's exemption, and the variety of arguments produced by registrary Tabor and others may have owed something to consultation of the archives. On the other hand the same arguments could equally well have emerged from perusal of Hare's collections and other books of precedents in the register office. Secondly, the Commission of 1639 appointed to draw up a roll of benefactors for annual commemoration certainly received instructions to explore the archives of the university and the final list mentions 'one hundred and thirty royal charters (more or less) reposing in the archives'. For the contents of these charters and for the names of private benefactors the sources again seem to have been volumes in the register office, the statutes, the Grace Books, and Hare. To the latter's transcription of the fictitious 'carte antique' from his contemporaries we probably owe the inclusion of such worthies as Sigebert, Offa, and King Alfred, in the Roll of Benefactors read for the first time in October, 1640.[1]

[1] Order of Service for the Commemoration of Benefactors, no. 1, fos. 7 and 8 (plate 4).

The next two decades brought their own pressing problems to the university and colleges, and it is not surprising that no public concern for the ancient muniments is manifested until after the Restoration. On 4 July 1662, however, a lengthy and important Grace concerning the archives was passed by the senate to the following effect:

> Since it contributes greatly to the honour and safety of the University that royal charters, acts of the Senate and our other public muniments should be solemnly kept in a safe place, which muniments hitherto have lain in townsmen's houses, exposed to fire, theft and many other mischances; May it please you that in the future they shall be kept in the Public Schools, and that under the auspices of the Vice-Chancellor a public repository for the University shall be built...where these muniments may be kept more securely and conveniently for the use of the Senate.[1]

That some documents had already strayed into private hands is known from the pre-Civil War period, but the wording of the Grace, 'inter oppidanorum aedes', suggests that the university muniments, like the university maces,[2] were deliberately left in the custody of individuals during the troubled years, although we have no record of any order given for the removal of the Chest from the vestry. Fears of a disturbance which might end in a disaster like that of 1381 were not groundless, for it was no further away than Peterborough that in 1643 a fanatical and ignorant soldiery had broken into the chapter house, deliberately destroying charters in the belief that they were papal bulls.[3] Whatever the exact nature of their dispersal under the Commonwealth, the need of a safe and permanent home for the archives was evident.

The place to which the archive repository was assigned by the Grace was 'a vacant space between the Schools of theology and philosophy', at the north-west corner of the Old Schools, under part of the room known as the Regent House. Here two small rooms were constructed, one panelled for the registrary's office,[4] the other 'fitted with strong bars and shelving' for the muniment room.[5]

By bringing the older muniments of the university into the same repository as the registers, the Grace of 1662 made almost inevitable the transfer of their custody

---

[1] Grace Book H, fo. 270. Printed in *Statuta Academiae Cantabrigiensis*, p. 394.

[2] A. P. Humphry, 'On the Maces of the Esquire Bedells and the Mace formerly borne by the Yeoman Bedell'. *Camb. Ant. Soc. Proc.* vol. IV (O.S.), no. XVI, pp. 207–19.

[3] Reginald L. Poole, *A Lecture on the History of the University Archives*, p. 23.

[4] University Audit Book, 1660–1740, fo. 15.

[5] For details of this reconstruction in the north-west corner of the Old Schools see Willis and Clark, *Architectural History*, vol. III, p. 23.

to the registrary. For the first time in their history all the muniments and papers of the university were to be kept in one place under the supervision of the same permanent official. Here was a golden opportunity for arranging and cataloguing the whole body of the archives, so that Cambridge no longer needed to fear comparison with Oxford in this respect. Oxford university had already led the way in the field of archive preservation with the appointment in 1634 of Brian Twyne as the first keeper of the archives. He and his successor, Langbaine, had done notable work in listing and arranging the documents in spite of the severe political disturbance of the times. In the years following the Restoration, Dr John Wallis, the third keeper and a Cambridge man, was compiling what was to remain the standard catalogue for the best part of three centuries.[1] Unfortunately for Cambridge, however, Whinn was not a man of this calibre, nor were his successors of the next half-century notable for zeal or even particular efficiency with the records. Indeed, it may be doubted whether the transfer of the older muniments from the vestry was completed by 1715, for in this year two Graces were passed, repeating the need for removing the records to the room adapted for that purpose and the proper ordering and arranging of the documents.[2] The alterations in the Old Schools necessitated by the arrival of the royal library at this date probably account for the revived interest in the muniments, and indeed the second Grace is preceded by one dealing with the problem of the large accession of books. To make room for them, both the New Chapel and the vestry had to be cleared, for we learn that by 1719, 'His Majesty's generous present of books rendered it necessary to increase the space in the Library by the addition of the New Chapel'.[3] It was not until Lynford Caryl (later master of Jesus College) was registrary (1751–8) that a catalogue was compiled. Caryl's catalogue is really a detailed inventory of the contents of each drawer or box as he found it; there is no attempt at classification. But at least he numbered each document carefully and listed them accordingly, and his work is still of some use today.

The Cambridge archives were unfortunate in their repository as well as in their keepers during the period, for the quarters provided in 1662 were both inadequate and damp. Plans for a new registry office figured in various building schemes in which the university was engaged after the completion of the Senate House but

[1] Reginald L. Poole, *A Lecture on the History of the University Archives*, p. 25.
[2] Grace Book Θ, fos. 640 and 654.   [3] Willis and Clark, *Architectural History*, vol. III, p. 34.

which, owing to controversy, and shortage of funds, did not materialise. Perhaps the most interesting of these plans were those of John Soane, in response to the following instructions:

13 April 1791. At a meeting of the Syndics...it was agreed that Mr Soane be desired to distribute the Interior space of the said intended Building into the following Rooms, viz: A musæum, a picture-gallery, a large Lecture Room, which may serve also for a Music Room, a smaller Lecture Room, and a Registrary's Office, and to lay his plan before the said Syndics as soon as he can conveniently.

His designs, which are still preserved in the university archives, were submitted to the senate on 13 December 1791, but were rejected without any recorded reason by a majority of two votes. After this, the plan for a new building was abandoned and with it any hope of a new home for the archives.[1]

By 1831 the registrary, William Hustler, realising that there was no prospect of a new permanent registry in the near future, expressed grave concern at the state of the records, and urged the consideration of a temporary expedient.[2] The report of the syndicate appointed to examine the matter was disquieting. The room was 'very unsatisfactory...imperfectly warmed and ventilated. Many of the documents (some of them of modern date) have been quite destroyed by damp, and many others will shortly be illegible, unless they are removed to a more proper place'. It was recommended that the former combination room in the Old Court of King's College, recently purchased by the university, should be fitted temporarily as a record room.[3] This room was at the extreme eastern end of the King's buildings and it was planned to seal it off from the rest of the block and effect a new entrance from the Law Schools. The plan proved neither so easy nor so cheap as the syndics had expected, for the Old Schools were built in two stories and the King's Old Court in three, with the combination room in the second.[4] To meet this difficulty, Hustler notes, a floor had to be raised, and a further £20 had to be added to the £60 already voted by Grace to cover the cost.[5] The only saving which was made was for the item 'servants for removing papers from old office'. Instead of the estimated £2 they got 12s.[6] The alterations and removal to the new room were completed shortly before Hustler's death in March 1832,

[1] Willis and Clark, *Architectural History*, vol. III, p. 74.   [2] Grace Book N, fo. 339.
[3] Grace Book N, fo. 347.
[4] Loggan's View of the Old Court of King's College, reproduced in Willis and Clark, *Architectural History*, vol. III, p. 80, fig. 14.
[5] Grace Book N, fo. 367.   [6] C.U.R. 20.1 (Registry), no. 15 (3–5).

but the records were not long in their new home. In 1836, order was given for the demolition of the Old Court of King's. Still hoping that a new office would eventually be built, the university decided, as a temporary measure, to accommodate the registry in a room on the ground floor of the newly built Pitt Press, and a Grace to this effect was passed on 2 March 1836.[1] These quarters were rather cramped and, in 1846, the syndics offered to exchange a room in the tower for the one on the ground floor. Joseph Romilly,[2] Hustler's successor, evidently approved of the change, for a note of his in the registry papers runs 'Removed to the noble room (built for a Press-Syndics-Room) in the tower of the Pitt Press— 8 November 1848. J.R.'[3]

Although intended as a temporary home only, the tower of the Pitt Press in fact housed the registrary and records for nearly a century. As a storage-place it was proof against damp but not against fire. When a serious fire broke out at the Pitt Press on 8 November 1893, the documents were only saved by being hastily flung out of the windows. It is probable that the archives were then housed for a time in the Old Library at Pembroke College (where the master and fellows had offered the registry a temporary refuge),[4] and were returned to the Pitt Press when it had been repaired and fitted with a strong-room. These improvements were the outcome of recommendations made by the syndicate, appointed by Grace on 23 November 1893, to consider how better provision could be made for the safe keeping of the records.[5] Apart from the fire episode, however, the archives during their sojourn in the Pitt Press had been better cared for than at any previous time in their history. Joseph Romilly of Trinity College, registrary from 1832 to 1862, had rescued the archives from the neglect and indifference of nearly two centuries, and by careful reading of them, indexing and annotation, had made them usable and intelligible for reference. His work was absolutely invaluable and can hardly be too highly praised. His successors, H. R. Luard (registrary, 1862–91) and J. W. Clark (registrary, 1891–1910), were both notable scholars and antiquaries who used the university archives for research and in published

[1] Grace Book N, fo. 540.
[2] Joseph Romilly (1791–1864) was the first cousin of John, first Baron Romilly (1802–74) who, as Master of the Rolls (1851–73), inaugurated the 'Rolls Series' of sources of medieval history.
[3] C.U.R. 20.1 (Registrary), no. 16.
[4] C.U.R. 20.2 (Registrary), no. 103 (letter of 9 November 1893).
[5] *Cambridge University Reporter*, 28 November 1893, p. 237.

works, and encouraged others to do so. The editing of the Grace Books A and B was a memorial to H. R. Luard.

After the first decade of this century, the archives again began to suffer an eclipse. The expansion of the university brought a corresponding increase in the business of the registrary's office and modern matters took priority over ancient. The registrary was no longer able to give personal supervision to the care of the archives, and in time the shelves became crowded with unwanted office material. The issue of the *Cambridge University Reporter* (first in 1870), and an increasing use of typescript and printed forms, meant that the new material had little affinity with the old. In any case, acts of parliament without, and statute revision within, had so altered the constitution and jurisdiction of the university that the scope and content of the archives was radically changed and many of the ancient series brought to an abrupt end. Once again, when no longer needed for current references, the archives were allowed to fall into a state of dirt and confusion. The removal of the university library to its new site in 1934 enabled the registry to move from its overcrowded quarters in the Pitt Press to its present place in the Old Schools. The archives were moved also, but again were put into temporary storage. Finally, in 1946–7, a proper strong-room was constructed in the court of the Old Schools and thus the university archives have come to rest within a few yards of their historic home. In 1949, with the aid of a sum given by the University Press, an honorary archivist to the university was appointed, together with an assistant archivist to restore order in the strong-room and to make the records available for reference and research. In 1953 the posts were established under the titles of keeper and deputy keeper of the archives, and from 1954 the full cost of maintaining the archives was placed on the University Chest. These changes did not deprive the registrary of his ultimate responsibility for the archives, and on the death of the first keeper in 1958, the council did not think it necessary to appoint another keeper in an honorary capacity. They therefore proposed that the full-time officer should henceforward be called the keeper of the archives.

PART II

4. THE UNIVERSITY AND COLLEGES AS PRIVILEGED CORPORATIONS

University and colleges, being alike autonomous, corporate bodies, have, as their corporate designation, either 'the Chancellor, Masters and Scholars of the University' or 'the Master, Fellows and Scholars' of the college. Each, therefore, has its own constitution and corpus of statutes, its own officials and servants, its own property and revenues. Each is the custodian of its own charters of privilege, title-deeds, and administrative records. Certain classes of documents will therefore be common to both university and colleges and, indeed, to most ancient corporations. Of these, the early charters and statutes are particularly important, in that they determine the nature of the university and colleges as privileged corporations.

CHARTERS OF PRIVILEGE

In a college muniment room, the most valued of the ancient charters is usually the foundation charter. The university differs from the colleges in having no such document and, indeed, no known founder. The university does not even possess the first authentic recognition of its existence by the crown, a small writ of 1231, concerning the rents of houses of scholars, which is recorded in the Close Rolls.[1] The earliest surviving document in the university archives is a letters patent of 1266, on the same subject, the first in the existing series of royal privileges granted to the university. The vicissitudes of fortune suffered by the university's early muniments have left them a less impressive collection than that of the sister university of Oxford or those of many institutions of comparable antiquity. To explain this state of affairs, great emphasis has been laid on the riots of 1381, when many of the early muniments were burnt. Some certainly perished, but in

---

[1] Close Rolls for 1227–31, pp. 586–7.

fact there remain to this day more than thirty royal charters, letters, and mandates, as well as several ecclesiastical and other documents, which date from before 1381. More damaging to the surviving charters than fire have been the ravages of damp and neglect over a long period, followed in the last century by repairs with unsuitable materials, folding into too small a compass, and even, in the case of some of the royal charters, the severing by knife of the laces by which the Great Seal was attached.

Nevertheless, many interesting and splendid documents remain. A list of charters of privilege and other documents from 1266 to 1544, formerly kept in the registry and now in the university archives, was published by registrary Luard in 1876.[1] For convenience, his system of enumeration is still retained, as it has been used in publications, and the following principal additions have been made:

No. 82a. 'Supplicaciones ad Curiam Romanam super etate et pluralitate beneficiorum.' Wm. Colville. Canc. c. 1390.

Nos. 148, 148a. 'Liber de fundacione exequiarum pro Rege Henrico VII', 20 November 1504, and 'Liber de fundacione exequiarum pro Domina Margareta', 2 March 1506.

No. 158a. 'Draft of the Surrender of the Charters, Privileges and Statutes of the University to Cardinal Wolsey, to alter and enlarge them as he shall think fit.' 18 April 1524.

The majority of the medieval muniments listed by Luard are royal grants and mandates or documents of ecclesiastical privilege, although he includes a certain amount of ancient miscellanea, petitions, licences, bonds, and letters. He also prints (in square brackets) entries from the catalogue of 1420 for other documents which had disappeared from the archives by 1876.

Of the royal benefactors in the medieval period Richard II was the most active, and twenty-seven of his grants or missives are extant. The earliest ecclesiastical charter is that of Bishop Hugo of Ely in 1276, limiting the jurisdiction of the archdeacon of Ely. The most interesting and important documents relating to ecclesiastical privilege are those connected with the Barnwell Process of 1430. Among them are the obviously spurious bulls of Sergius I and Honorius I, by which the university sought to substantiate its claim for exemption from episcopal and archiepiscopal jurisdiction, and the genuine, gold-lettered bull of Eugenius IV (18 September 1433) by which the privilege was actually conferred in the form of a confirmation.[2] There are also a few compositions with colleges and other bodies, and the earliest of these which survives is the important composition of 1270 with the town, arbitrated by the Lord Edward and confirmed by the crown. Another

---

[1] *Camb. Antiq. Soc. Proc.* vol. III (O.S.), no. XXXVIII (pp. 387–403). [2] Plate 5.

interesting composition is that made with the mendicant orders at Bordeaux in 1306, and this has a beautiful and possibly unique seal, representing St Dominic and St Francis. Two documents of 1426 also relate to the Franciscans.

For the period 1546 to 1771/2 there are a further eighteen royal charters, confirmations of charters, and letters patent.[1] The greatest royal patrons of the university in this period were Elizabeth I and James I (whereas at the university of Oxford the comprehensive charter of Charles I takes pride of place). A copy of the 'Index to the Great Register in the University Chest' and the text of some of the more important charters up to the reign of James I, based mainly on Hare's transcripts (see chapter 9), were published by G. Dyer, *The Privileges of the University of Cambridge* (1824). The charters and letters patent of Elizabeth I and James I were published, after collation with the original documents, by registrary J. W. Clark in 1892, and the same editor's *Endowments of the University of Cambridge* (1904) gives the text of most of the remaining later charters of privilege.

STATUTES

Next in importance to the charters themselves are the statutes, which also bear witness to the status of the university and colleges as privileged corporations. Many of the colleges possess an original or early copy of the statutes given by their founders. Some of them (Clare, Pembroke, Trinity Hall) also deposited early copies in the University Chest, which are still extant. Until recently, it was thought that the university had no complete corpus of statutes earlier than about the last decade of the fourteenth century, in a copy probably written to replace those destroyed in the fire. In 1957, however, an Irish scholar, the Rev. Dr Benedict Hackett, O.S.A., while working at Rome in a library once belonging to his order, came upon a late thirteenth-century manuscript with the title 'Constitutiones Universitatis Cantebrigie' containing what appears to be a complete collection of the early statutes of Cambridge. The first item concerns the election and office of chancellor, and the last deals with the obsequies for deceased members of the university and their benefactions. The majority of these very early statutes are incorporated in the extant collections of later date.[2] It is interesting to note

---

[1] These include grants of arms in the form of letters patent issued by Robert Cooke, Clarencieux King of Arms (plates 6 and 7).   [2] M. D. Knowles in a letter to *The Times* of 23 December 1957.

that Dr Hackett has examined an unprinted manuscript containing a very full inventory of the contents of the Augustinian library, dated 1478. There is no mention in it of the manuscript which contains the Cambridge statutes. Consequently it may be taken as certain that the manuscript was not acquired before 1478. Dr Hackett is now preparing this manuscript collection of statutes (which is probably unique) for publication by the University Press.

The statutes of the medieval period were authorised by the university itself, and recorded by the proctors. The earliest collection of statutes in the university archives formed the Old Proctor's Book (or 'Fragmenta Vetera'), which was made about 1390.[1] Some of the folios of this book were later removed, and rebound in the Junior Proctor's Book. These early statutes were added to from time to time, until 1570, when the great Elizabethan code of statutes[2] became the new foundation of university government. This code, and subsequent ones, derive their authority from the crown, and in their turn were added to and interpreted until the next complete revisions in 1858 and 1882.[3] Most of the college statutes followed a similar course of development and were also given a Victorian overhaul. The latest wholesale revision of statutes was in 1926. The most notable printed editions of the unreformed statutes are those of 1785 and 1852. The statutes produced under the act of 1877 were published in 1882, and since then there have been frequent new editions, with supplements published between editions, of the statutes and ordinances. The archives contain, in addition to statutes and early grants, printed acts of parliament and orders in council relating to the university. Many transcripts of the early statutes have been made at various dates.

5. RECORDS OF UNIVERSITY ADMINISTRATION

The continuous administrative records of the university begin in 1454 with the series of Grace Books, which extends unbroken to 1880. The earliest Grace Books, A and B, contain the undifferentiated records of University business, both financial

---

[1] Plate 1; and see *Documents relating to the University and Colleges of Cambridge*, vol. 1, p. 306.
[2] Plate 8.   [3] D. A. Winstanley, *Early Victorian Cambridge* (Cambridge, 1940), pp. 234–69 and 314–38.

and administrative, from 1454 to 1500, and were kept by the proctors. They are sometimes called by their earlier title, 'Registra Procuratorum'. After 1500, the proctors continued to keep their annual financial records in Grace Book B, until the book was filled in 1544, and thereafter in a separate series of audit books. The other administrative business of the university, chiefly in the form of 'Graces of the Senate', was recorded in a new register, Grace Book Γ. This register is, from its inception in 1501, kept by one person, the hand not changing annually as in the 'Registra Procuratorum', and its writer and custodian was probably Robert Hobbys, esquire bedell, who became the first registrary in 1506. From this date until 1880, the Grace Books were kept by the registrary. Grace Books A and B, covering the period 1454–1544, have been published in the Luard Memorial Series by the Cambridge Antiquarian Society, and Grace Books Γ and Δ, covering the period 1501–89, have been published by the Cambridge University Press. The introductions to this series of published Grace Books form an invaluable commentary on the volumes themselves, and on the administration which produced them. They show, among other things, how the 'Grace', originally a personal exemption from statutory requirements granted by the senate to those aspiring to a degree, came to serve wider and more general purposes. From the fifteenth century, degrees became increasingly 'gratiosi' rather than 'rigorosi' and the Grace Books therefore provide what is virtually a register of degrees. From the end of the same century, the Grace formula came to be used for other persons and matters, the first instance being the Grace for the bedells of 1483–4, which has been described as 'something between a Grace and a Statute'. By the mid-sixteenth century, the Grace was an established procedure for a great variety of executive business, which the senate wished to authorise, but which was not of sufficient importance or permanence to require a statute. From the sixteenth century also, original letters and contemporary copies of various documents relating to university affairs are from time to time incorporated in the Grace Books.

By the early nineteenth century, the practice of copying a long report to the senate into the Grace Book in order to explain the subsequent Grace had made the volumes increasingly bulky and awkward for reference, as well as adding greatly to the labours of the registrary. A partial solution to the problem was found by placing the relevant reports, letters, or other documents relating to a projected Grace, separately on the registrary's table. If discussion was anticipated, these documents were sometimes printed and circulated as fly-sheets. This additional material was filed in the registry and remains in the archives.

The *Cambridge University Reporter* printed by C. J. Clay at the University Press, and published every Wednesday during term time by Messrs Rivington, 19 Trinity Street, Cambridge, as a private venture, first appeared on 19 October 1870. The prospectus declared that the *Reporter* had no party purpose to serve and aimed at affording an opportunity for open discussion in all subjects fairly connected with the interests of the university.[1] The last number published by Rivington's appeared on 18 December 1872. The circulation among non-residents had been disappointing and publication was transferred to the syndics of the University Press on the understanding that the insertion of letters and original matter would be discontinued. In December 1872 the syndics appointed as editor George Forrest Browne of St Catharine's, the paper's former editor, at a stipend of £100 per annum.[2] From 14 January 1873, the *Cambridge University Reporter*, published by authority, has been the official record of university administration. The contents of the *Reporter* are divided into two parts, the 'official' and the 'unofficial'. In the former are recorded the names of recipients of degrees, appointments to university offices and posts, notices of discussions due to take place in the Senate House, members elected or co-opted to various committees or faculty boards, awards to scholarships, exhibitions and prizes, grants for travel and research, examination results, reports of various university departments, obituary notices, 'Graces' for the next congregation, 'Graces' sanctioned and degrees conferred at the previous congregation, and other matters of university interest. In the second or 'unofficial' part of the *Reporter* are found college notices, notices of forthcoming meetings of learned societies, notices of vacant posts at Oxford, other universities, and similar institutions, and reprints of fly-sheets.

While official acts of the university have always been recorded in Graces of the senate, there has also for several centuries been a small executive body at the centre of university administration. Under the statutes of 1570, the 'caput' filled the role. These statutes laid down that all Graces submitted to the senate had first to be approved by the 'caput'. It was a small body consisting of the chancellor,

---

[1] Rt Rev. G. F. Browne, *The Recollections of a Bishop* (London, 1915), pp. 121–4.
[2] S. C. Roberts, *The Evolution of Cambridge Publishing* (The Sandars Lectures for 1954, Cambridge, 1956), pp. 36 and 37.

three doctors, and a regent and non-regent master, elected annually by the heads of houses and doctors from names on lists submitted by the chancellor and proctors.[1] No detailed records, either of these elections or of the 'caput' itself, have been preserved. As a result of its deliberations, letters and orders were issued from time to time by the vice-chancellor, and these are normally recorded in the Grace Books. Other orders were issued under the combined authority of the vice-chancellor and heads. Such as survived in loose sheets, from 1574, were bound into a guard-book in 1870. In some cases the original order is preserved, with draft amendments and signatures. Regulations affecting the whole university were usually printed as broadsheets, for distribution in the colleges and posting in the public buildings of the university. Notebooks of 'Orders of Vice-Chancellor and Heads' were kept from 1750.

The 'caput' passed out of existence on 6 November 1856, and the election of the first council of the senate took place on 7 November 1856. The council consisted of the chancellor, vice-chancellor, four heads of colleges, four professors of the university, and eight other members of the senate to be chosen from the electoral roll, such heads of colleges, professors and members of the senate being elected by the persons whose names are on the electoral roll. The earlier volumes of council minutes are kept in the archives, and the more recent ones in the university registry. They run from November 1856 to date.

6. RECORDS OF MATRICULATION AND DEGREES

Two groups in the archives relate to matriculations. First, there are the Praelectors' Lists, submitted to the registrary by the individual colleges, which are very rough and usually undated. These survive from about 1589. Secondly, the registrary or his clerk compiled from these lists the Matriculation Registers, which run from 1544, when matriculation was instituted by statute, to the present day. From 1724

[1] J. P. C. Roach, 'The University of Cambridge', *Victoria County History of Cambridgeshire*, vol. III, pp. 183–4. Also *The Historical Register of the University of Cambridge...to the Year 1910*, ed. J. R. Tanner (Cambridge, 1917), pp. 3–4.

an undergraduate signed his own name in the registers. Matriculation was the occasion of his taking the oath of fidelity to his Alma Mater, a ceremony, says Venn,[1] 'presumably of very ancient origin, although there are no extant records of the ceremony earlier than this date' (that is, 1544). Students under the age of fourteen did not have to take the oath. They are distinguished by the word 'impubes'. The Matriculation Registers are the only official record of membership of the university, but unfortunately present some inaccuracies, and there are also several omissions. Many names of students who undoubtedly came into residence are omitted altogether. For the period 1590–1601, no matriculations have been recorded at all, owing to the negligence of the then registrary.

The principal record of degrees conferred is in the Graces listed in the Grace Books. From 1498/9 the Graces for each degree are normally supplemented in the Grace Books by the annual 'Ordo Senioritatis', which was later replaced by the printed Tripos Lists.[2] From 1491/2 to 1497/8, miscellaneous lists of the 'Ordo' survive. It is impossible to say on what grounds the arrangement was originally made; in many cases priority was certainly granted to social position: the fellow-commoner, or young man of family, often stands first.[3] In other cases, as in that of Dr John Caius, in 1532/3, it looks as if intellectual pre-eminence was the determining cause. A short account of the gradual evolution of the ancient 'Ordo' into the later 'Tripos' is given in the introduction to Grace Book Δ. The names of graduates given in the Grace Books are supplemented by the 'Supplicats' (1568–1870), in which the college concerned certified to the senate the candidates' qualifications and requested that the degree be conferred. Normally, the 'Supplicats' duplicate the degree lists but, in a very few instances, they contain the names of those who attempted the final test but who do not subsequently appear in the degree lists.

The names of graduates are also found in autograph in the series of Subscription Books from 1616. Subscription records actually begin in 1613, when at the command of James I the senate passed a decree by Grace of 7 July 1613, requiring all holders of superior degrees to subscribe to the 'Three Articles of Religion'. (The original Grace setting out the 'Three Articles' in full is in front of the first

[1] John and J. A. Venn, *Alumni Cantabrigienses*, pt. 1, vol. 1, p. vi.
[2] *The Historical Register of the University of Cambridge...to the year 1910*, ed. J. R. Tanner.
[3] Plate 10. Note position of John North in the 'Ordo'.

register.) Subscription for inferior degrees was enjoined by His Majesty on 3 December 1616 in a mandate of which the signed original is preserved in the archives. Subscription continued to be exacted in this form until 1640–1, when the practice was suppressed by the House of Commons. On the restoration of King Charles II, subscription to the 'Three Articles' was renewed by order of the King.[1] Opposition to the 'test' of subscription grew in the nineteenth century, coming to a head in the struggles of 1833–4. As a result of these, the form was changed to a declaration of being 'a bona fide member of the Established Church' by the statutory commission of 1856. In 1871 the tests in both the universities were abolished by the passing of the Universities Tests Act. A description of the earlier practices with regard to subscription was issued by G. Ainslie, master of Pembroke College, in 1833, entitled 'An Historical Account of the Oaths and Subscriptions required in the University of Cambridge on Matriculation and of all persons who proceed to the Degree of Master of Arts'. A modern account of the later struggles, based on material in the university archives, is given in D. A. Winstanley's *Early Victorian Cambridge* and *Later Victorian Cambridge*. Until towards the end of 1934, all recipients of degrees signed their names in a so-called 'Subscription Register' but, following a resolution of the council of the senate, this practice ceased after that date.[2] The signatures of persons who receive honorary degrees are now entered in a volume on their own.

Degrees by mandate, that is, degrees awarded upon the receipt of letters of recommendation, were not unknown in the medieval period. The earliest letter of this kind in the university archives is that from Thomas Beaufort, Duke of Exeter, shortly before the session of the General Council of Constance, held in May 1416. He writes,

To the which Conseil at his Mandement schul go certain prelates of this Rewme in whos Companie we desire to sende over ouer welbeloved Clerk Maistre Guy Wiseham the whom er his going for that cause and the worschip of the universite that he is studiant of, and of himself bothe, we desire in cas he were able, to be graduat unto the degre of Bacheler of the faculte in which he is and hath be studying.[3]

The practice was much extended in the following century, both the sovereign, and those holding high office in the realm, sending mandates and letters for degrees and also for university offices to be given to their followers. Unlike

---

[1] [Gilbert Ainslie], *Oaths and Subscriptions* (Cambridge, 1833), p. 55.
[2] Minutes of the Council of the Senate, 12 and 19 February 1934.
[3] Transcribed by H. R. Luard in *Camb. Ant. Soc. Proc.* vol. III (O.S.), no. XXV, p. 273 (1872).

master Wiseham, few of these persons were already studying at Cambridge, or even had pretensions to learning at all. The personal interference of notable courtiers in the award of the university honours was at its greatest during the reign of Elizabeth I, and letters from Burghley, Sir Walter Raleigh, Cecil and others, to this end, may be found in the series of original Letters and Mandates for Degrees, preserved in the university archives, for the reigns of Elizabeth I–James II. In the following reigns, however, royal mandates gradually superseded those of subjects, and the lists for mandate degrees grew somewhat unwieldy, especially on the occasions of royal visits. In fact, so numerous and so unsuitable did the recipients become, that by 1688 the whole practice of mandate degrees had fallen into contempt. Shortly after the Revolution, it was agreed between the crown and the university that the sovereign should only issue letters mandatory at the receipt of a petition from the chancellor, and that the chancellor should not petition unless he had received a certificate, signed by the majority of the heads of houses, recommending the applicant as intellectually qualified.[1] During the reign of Charles I, the mandate degree was very occasionally conferred upon persons who were not required to make the Subscription (the degree given to Peter Paul Rubens being a case in point), but this practice did not survive the stricter regulations against nonconformity (and particularly Roman Catholicism) enforced after the Revolution. It was not until 1851 that the statutes revision syndicate recommend that

foreigners of distinction, rank, or talent, and natives of the United Kingdom of Great Britain and Ireland, distinguished by talent or public service, may be admitted to titular degrees of honour in arts, law, or physic, without being called upon to make any subscription or affirmation, provided that none of these persons shall by virtue of such admission have any vote in the Senate.[2]

By an interpretation of the Elizabethan statutes, extended by a royal letter of Charles II, the university was able to confer degrees upon various categories of 'honourable persons' and their sons. Among these 'privilege degrees' was the M.A., which could be granted to persons if related to the sovereign by consanguinity or affinity.[3] A few pedigrees specially making this claim, some beautifully inscribed and in their original boxes, remain in the university archives to testify to this curious privilege. One with considerable historical interest is that

[1] D. A. Winstanley, *Unreformed Cambridge* (Cambridge, 1935), p. 85.
[2] D. A. Winstanley, *Early Victorian Cambridge* (Cambridge, 1940), pp. 246–7.   [3] *Ibid.* pp. 152–3.

of a member of the Penn family. Degrees to 'honourable persons' were abolished by a Grace of 18 March 1825.

Degrees by incorporation have their separate entries in the Grace Books and also in the Subscription Registers until near the end of 1934, when signatures for degrees were no longer obligatory. The archives contain a certain number of old degree certificates of Oxford and Trinity College, Dublin, sent in by those desiring to incorporate.

7. FINANCIAL RECORDS OF THE UNIVERSITY

Under the medieval constitution, the proctors had been the most important administrative officers in the university and, as such, were responsible for finance. By the statute of 1570, many of the proctorial functions, including financial control, were transferred either to the chancellor or to the vice-chancellor, and the office thus lost much of its ancient importance. The first statement of the university's financial position in medieval times is found in a series of Proctors' Indentures, the earliest of which is dated 1363.[1] As has been stated in an earlier chapter (chapter 5), Grace Books A and B both contain detailed financial and other records, dating from 1454 to 1500. After the latter date, annual financial records only were kept in Grace Book B and, after 1544, a separate series of Audit Books came into existence. The accounts in these early Grace Books are very varied in their content and scope, and do not follow any particular arrangement. Outgoings and receipts, cautions, accounts of certain benefactions and tables of degrees are grouped together in rather a haphazard way.

The financial records of this period are of immense interest, shedding fresh light on historical events, and on the part played by the university in religious and political matters. This is especially true of the accounts of the Reformation period, showing as they do 'the University treating on the one part with Henry VIII, Wolsey and Cromwell, and, on the other with enraged and excommunicated Mayors and bailiffs'.[2] It is interesting to note here that, although the Proctors'

---

[1] See p. 1 and plate 9.   [2] Introduction to *Grace Book* B (Cambridge, 1905), pt. II, p. viii.

Accounts often confirm the details of the conflicts between the university and town, as known from other sources, they do not appear to include an account of the fines levied by them in Sturbridge Fair. Various other aspects of university activities are reflected in these accounts; for example the influence of the Reformation is shown by certain entries, the most striking of these being at the end of the Easter term, 1521, where a charge is entered for drink and expenses at the burning of Luther's books. An entry of a later date shows that the goodwill of Thomas Cromwell had been sought by a payment of a stipend of £2 a year for life. In addition, a few financial entries reflect changes in the university regulations, and the payment of certain lecturers are also noted. During these years, the financial resources of the university were at a very low ebb, and the balance of the Chest much reduced. This state of affairs may partly be accounted for by the diminishing number of degrees taken. In addition, the university had incurred heavy legal expenses in 1532–3 in its conflicts with the town. Indeed, by 1544, the proctors were faced with a small deficit.

The important series of Audit Books which is to be found in the university archives begins in 1545 and continues until 1880, although there is a gap for the years 1822–8. It is interesting to note the usual form of these early Audit Books. Each financial year begins with a general account of the Chest, and then follow the two smaller accounts of the senior and junior proctor, audited by the vice-chancellor and three other persons (the proctors' financial year ran from Michaelmas to Michaelmas). They are followed by the Vice-Chancellor's Account, the financial year in this instance covering the period from 3 November to 3 November. This account is divided into two parts, first, the 'Recepta' or incoming monies, to which are added cautions received, and secondly, 'Expenses' or disbursements, which are subdivided into: (a) 'Expenses Certain' (salaries, wages and so on), to which are added cautions returned; (b) 'Expenses Uncertain' (variable annual expenses) and 'Expenses Extraordinary'. Later, subsidiary accounts develop independently, such as those connected with the Rustat Benefaction and the University Press. Where a benefaction was administered by a separate trust, the latter kept its own accounts. Similarly, when an *ad hoc* syndicate or committee was appointed with powers to administer special funds, separate accounts were kept, and both these types of accounts remain in the archives.

The university Audit Books are supplemented by a series of bound volumes of university vouchers for the period 1558–1700, and also a large number of un-bound Vice-Chancellor's Accounts and vouchers for 1575–1859. These include receipts for expenses of all kinds incurred by the university.

On the introduction of the new statutes of 1882, the care and management of the property and income of the university passed to the Financial Board and it was also decided that the financial year of the university should in future terminate each year on 31 December. The first accounts published by the Financial Board were for the period 3 November 1881 to 31 December 1882. Up to and including 1919 the financial year ended on 31 December, but this date was altered in 1920 to 30 September and again in 1923 to 31 July, and this date is still in operation today. Over this period there appears to be little change in the presentation of the accounts. The main changes seem to be in the greatly increased number of accounts and the sums of money involved. The modern ledgers and also the cash books from 1852 are at present kept in the Financial Board offices.

It should be noted that each department of the university is responsible for its own expenditure, and therefore detailed records concerning its accounts are in the custody of the department concerned, and supplement the data available in the accounts kept by the Financial Board.

The main sources of university income are capital investments, Treasury grants, and private grants from outside bodies. Capital transactions relating either to land belonging to the university or to the investments representing capital arising from dealings in land are subject to the supervision of the Ministry of Agriculture, Fisheries and Food, and all such investments have to be registered in the name of the Minister in accordance with the provisions of the Universities and College Estates Act, 1925. This act replaces provisions in a series of statutes dating back to the reign of Elizabeth I. All these dealings are recorded in the files at present in the Financial Board offices.

No account of the records of university finance in recent years would be complete without mention of the assistance which is now given to universities by the Treasury, through the recommendations of the University Grants Committee. The recurrent grants made through the University Grants Committee are based on a five-year period. Every five years the university has to submit to the chairman of the University Grants Committee estimates of the cost of continuing current commit-ments, and proposals for new developments the university wishes to undertake during the following quinquennium. Proposals for new developments from faculty boards are 'edited' by the General Board, in preparation for a general statement of needs for the following quinquennium. The University Grants Committee makes its recommendations to the Treasury relating to the most important needs and announces its grants for the five years of the next quinquennium (subject to the provision of the necessary monies by parliament). Buildings are dealt with separately. The university submits an order of priority for new schemes and the University Grants Committee assesses a grant for each building independently. Copies of statements of needs, and many files of data and correspondence with the University Grants Committee are in the university offices, and much of this will, one day, be deposited with the archives. It should be noted also that a notice appears annually in the *Reporter*, showing the grants made in the previous financial year for research wholly or partly supported by funds from outside bodies.

8. ENDOWMENTS OF THE UNIVERSITY

It was customary in the medieval university for benefactors to be recompensed for their generosity in masses and prayers offered by the clerks of the university for the welfare of their souls. The earlier statutes recorded in the Proctors' Books contain several directed to this end, among them the statute of 1398 for Sir William Thorpe, in whose completed chapel many of the services for departed benefactors were to be held.[1] The calendars, with which the Proctors' Books are prefaced, have entered in them the days on which exequies of the more important benefactors were to be observed. In addition, the colleges had their own commemorations, and among the charters of the university are several compositions with a college to provide for joint performance of pious duties connected with a benefaction. As the number of benefactors increased, all could not be given special obituary services, and a form of annual commemoration was adopted, mentioning each by name only in a general bidding prayer. A late pre-Reformation form is given in Stokys' Book, dated by its exhortation (following the names of departed

[1] See chapter 1.

royal benefactors), 'et (orate) pro bono statu domini Henrici Octavi regis nostri et Katerine regine consortis sue'.[1]

The first decade of the sixteenth century brought to the university by far the most important of the benefactions made specifically to provide for the welfare of the donors' souls, those of King Henry VII and the Lady Margaret, his mother. Each takes the form of a lengthy tripartite indenture, in book form, sealed with the respective seals of the parties. That of Henry VII, dated 20 November 1504, ordains one form of service to be used annually during his lifetime, and another, observing his exequies and those of his family, to be celebrated for ever after his death. He himself provided the cloth-of-gold pall to be used on the sarcophagus; a cloth which had a chequered and fascinating post-Reformation history and which may still be seen in the Fitzwilliam Museum. Its counterpart is in the Ashmolean Museum at Oxford.[2] More important for the future history of the university, however, is the indenture of the Lady Margaret, written in English, and dated 2 March 1506. By its terms, the abbot of Westminster was endowed with certain lands, from which he had to pay an annual sum of twenty marks for the stipend of a reader in divinity, to be known as the Lady Margaret Reader; while the university, in its turn, covenanted to perform exequies. In this way, the first of the university's professorships was endowed. Two years later, the foundress settled an annual stipend upon a public preacher. By a somewhat similar tripartite agreement with Jesus College and the university, the executors of Sir Robert Rede, Chief Justice of the Common Pleas, founded in 1524 three annual lectureships (known later as the 'Barnaby Lectures'), in return for 'a solempne Anniversarie in Great Saint Marie's Church'.[3] They were later converted into the modern Rede Lecture. Although the religious observances for which these benefactions were made did not survive the Reformation, their scholastic provisions laid an enduring foundation for the succession of professorships, readerships and lectureships with which the university has subsequently been endowed.

After the Reformation, a new type of religious commemoration was instituted when, in March 1559, the executors of John Mere arranged in his memory an

[1] 'Stokys' Book', fo. 24b.

[2] H. Tait, 'The Hearse-cloth of Henry VII belonging to the University of Cambridge'. *Journal of the Warburg and Courtauld Institutes*, vol. XIX, nos. 3–4, pp. 294–8 (1956).

[3] C. P. Murrell, 'The Manor of Withyham and Sir Robert Rede'. *Sussex Arch. Soc. Notes and Queries*, vol. XIII, no. 4 (1950).

annual commemoration sermon in St Bene't's Church. The indenture for this sermon is in the university archives, although Mere's will and other papers relating to his benefactions are in Corpus Christi College.[1] No general form of commemoration was provided for university benefactors, however, until a commission was appointed in 1639 to draw up a roll of their names and a form of service.[2] With slight modifications, the service is that performed annually in our own day. Copies of the various editions of the roll of benefactors from 1639 are preserved in the archives.

In addition to the charters, indentures, or foundation deeds creating endowments, there are in the university archives muniments of title relating to any real property which formed a part of the endowment, and papers relating to the management of the property and distribution of the income arising from it. As far as ancient muniments of title are concerned, however, the university archives are poor in comparison with those of the majority of the colleges. For the colleges were by far the greater owners of landed estates, and even the later foundations may possess valuable charters and manorial records, which have descended to them from dissolved monastic houses and ancient family estates. By contrast, according to Wren's catalogue of 1620, the university possessed only the site of the Old Schools, a few town houses, some farmland near Cambridge, and the advowson of Burwell. The earliest town property still in the possession of the university is incorporated into the site of the Old Schools. The earliest charter in the university archives relating to this site is a grant to Thomas Kelsal from the nuns of St Leonard, Stratford-at-Bow, in 1395, of a house in School Lane.[3] Rysley's inventory records deeds, unfortunately no longer extant, of the benefactions of Roger de Heydon and Nigel de Thornton. The latter, the donor of the greater part of the site of the Old Schools, also endowed the university chaplain with the rents of his 'lands' (or strips) in the open fields of Cambridge.[4] Papers relating to these 'university lands', and to the rents which continued to be collected from them up to the enclosure of the fields, are preserved in the archives from 1555 to 1703. Extensions to the original Old Schools site on the east and the west, made by purchase (principally from King's College) in the eighteenth and

---

[1] MS. 106, nos. 349 and 350 in Corpus Christi College.   [2] See p. 18 and plate 4.
[3] Document no. 77 (Luard's list). Discussed in Willis and Clark, *Architectural History*, vol. III, p. 7.
[4] H. P. Stokes, *The Chaplains and the Chapel of the University of Cambridge*, pp. 5–7.

early nineteenth century, brought to the archives muniments of title of the various properties which formerly occupied the site.

The most important of the town houses, of which the title deeds were catalogued by Wren, were the two adjoining houses in Bene't Street, bequeathed to the university by John Mere in 1558. From 1625, when a small garden on the opposite side of the street was added by gift from Mrs Alice Davers, the property was assigned to the use of the Lady Margaret professor. The houses were sold by the university in 1898 and are now the Bath Hotel. Shortly after Mere's bequest, Archbishop Parker, formerly master of Corpus Christi College, presented to the university a strip of land running from opposite Great St Mary's to the front of the Schools. The handsome tripartite indenture dated 6 August 1574, which is still in the university archives, is entitled 'Archbishop Parker's Gift of University Street', but the narrow lane (less than 25 feet wide) was popularly known as Regent Walk. A house on the south side of this lane was bequeathed in 1652-3 by John Crane, for the use of the regius professor of physic, as part of a larger benefaction directed to the support of sick scholars and other charitable purposes. When, in 1724, both Crane's house and Regent Walk were required for the site of the new Senate House, a house in Shoemaker Row (now Market Street) was exchanged by the university for the one in Regent Walk, and became the endowment of the physic professor. The premises are now occupied by Messrs Eaden Lilley. Deeds of Mere's houses are preserved in the archives from about 1362 to 1882, of Crane's house from 1599 to 1653, and of the house in Shoemaker Row (called indifferently 'The Crow' or 'Le Raven') from 1515 to 1753.

Title-deeds relating to later acquisitions in the city of Cambridge are not, at present, kept in the university archives, although some papers relating to the use of sites are found among the minutes of 'building' and other *ad hoc* syndicates.

The bulk of the university property lying outside the immediate environs of Cambridge was not acquired until the later seventeenth and eighteenth centuries, usually as an endowment for a teaching post, or a university scholarship or prize. Such property was, however, often vested in trustees, and not directly controlled by the university; as in the case of the Jacksonian professorship, where the master and fellows of Trinity College were appointed trustees for the administration of the estate. Sometimes, as in the case of the Rustat donation for the library, the university was appointed the trustee. A list of properties for which the university holds muniments of title and relevant papers is given in appendix B. Where no muniments of title are preserved for an old endowment, the likelihood is that they have been left in the custody of a trustee. In the nineteenth century and later, however, endowments have more frequently taken the form of monetary investments rather than that of landed estates. During recent years, the policy of the university (and, indeed, of many of the colleges) has been to sell its real property as opportunity presents itself, and to invest the proceeds elsewhere.

Publication of deeds of trust and deeds of foundation concerning teaching offices in the university was begun by William Webb, D.D., master of Clare College, who, in 1818, printed documents relating to the Plumian, Woodwardian and Lucasian professorships, and to the Arabic lectureship founded by Sir Thomas Adams.[1] In 1857 the Rev. Henry Philpott, D.D., master of St Catharine's College, published *Trusts, Statutes and Directions affecting the Professorships of the University*, followed by two small books relating to 'Scholarships, Prizes and to certain other Gifts and Endowments'. The preparation of new editions of university endowments subsequently became one of the responsibilities of the registrary, and the last complete edition to be published was that by registrary J. W. Clark, in 1904. A modern one is in course of preparation.

9. UNIVERSITY OFFICERS AND THEIR RECORDS

Although at the present day the bulk of university teaching and university administration is carried out by a staff of salaried officers, supported by a body of university assistants, this state of affairs is relatively modern. Unlike the teaching posts, which from the sixteenth century to the nineteenth century depended almost entirely upon endowments, many of the administrative offices, especially those of the greatest antiquity and honour, derive from periods when quite other modes of appointment and emolument were customary. Sufficient relics of these older systems, embedded in the modern, remain to give to university life and ceremonial

[1] J. W. Clark (ed.), *Endowments of the University of Cambridge* (Cambridge, 1904), p. v.

much of their distinctive quality, and to make the records of the various offices a rewarding subject of study. The offices have been of the greatest diversity, including graduate and non-graduate, resident and non-resident, and ranging from those of the highest honour, worthy to be held by magnates of the realm, to the humbler posts, such as those of the university plumber and pewterer. For convenience, they can be considered in a few general groups, according to the mode of appointment, tenure, and emoluments of office.

In the impecunious medieval university, the burden of office was, on the whole, expected to be heavier than the rewards, and a system was evolved by which office-holders changed annually or biennially. Appointment to administrative office was by election made according to forms prescribed in the statutes. Bonds against non-performance of duty were taken from persons entering upon their term of office and a detailed indenture between the outgoing officer and his successor served for the acquittance of the former. Office-holders originally received no stipends, though certain gifts and bequests might come their way, and reasonable expenses could be claimed. Similarly, every newly incepted master had to perform his statutory terms as a regent,[1] that is, one of the body of teaching masters, and bonds were exacted from any other teachers engaged to give special lectures.[2]

The oldest offices in the university, which still adhere to the medieval type of appointment and tenure (though, fortunately, not to the same system of emolument), are those of the vice-chancellor (originally chancellor) and proctors. These are the officers depicted upon the ancient seal of the university (1580), the chancellor, or vice-chancellor, being the head or president of the body of masters, and the proctors his executive officers. As these officers have been at the centre of university administration ever since its inception, their earlier records are, as has already been shown, the parents of all the main series of administrative, financial and judicial records of the university. Even after greater differentiation of function and wider distribution of duties had taken place, the records of vice-chancellor and proctors continue to bulk largely until modern times. Associated with the proctors in some of their duties[3] and elected in the same way were the taxors, whose

---

[1] G. Peacock, *Observations on the Statutes*, p. 19.

[2] Bond in £10 of Ralph, canon of Croxton, for reading lectures in canon law for three years (1392). Document no. 76 (Luard's list).   [3] G. Peacock, *Observations on the Statutes*, p. 24.

office has documentary evidence in the archives from the earliest extant university charter of 1266 to its abolition, following Sir John Patteson's award of 1855.

Records relating to the appointment and tenure of all these officers are numerous. From the medieval period there is the series of Proctors' Indentures, between the incoming and outgoing proctors, running consecutively from 1431 ro 1501. Financial records continue to supply most of our information about the proctors' office up to 1570. Voting-papers from the elections for vice-chancellor, proctors, and taxors are preserved from the mid-seventeenth century, while bonds of proctors and taxors run from the same period to 1882 and 1854 respectively. Miscellanea from the sixteenth to the nineteenth century, relating to details of the performance of office, controversies over rights and dignities of office, changes in emoluments and bills of expenses claimed, are bound into the guard-books C.U.R. 35 'Taxors'; C.U.R. 41 'Proctors'; C.U.R. 44 'Vice-Chancellor'. It must be noted, however, that there is very little personal material unrelated to the holding of office. Correspondence, even of an official character, beyond what was copied into letter-books and the Grace Books, has only been preserved from the Elizabethan period and the first decades of the seventeenth century, and in a few isolated cases from the nineteenth century.

An interesting but incomplete series, running only for some of the years 1553–83 and 1624–53, is that of the vice-chancellor's 'Tradita'. These documents, corresponding in form and purpose to the Proctors' Indentures at the annual change of officers, list the keys, seals, evidences and other valuables delivered by a retiring vice-chancellor to his successor. They include far more miscellaneous items than the modest key-ring which, with the Essex Cup, appears at the present-day ceremony on 1 October. The earlier indentures enumerate in detail books, letters, charters and a 'box of evidences relating to Burwell'. Later an independent list appears, entitled, 'A catalogue of books normally in the Vice-Chancellor's Cabinet, 1657', followed by a similar list in 1797. Foremost in the lists are the 'Old Vice-Chancellor's Book', a collection of statutes, graces, and other documents, originally made by Dr Perne and kept up to date until about 1645; and its successor, 'The Vice-Chancellor's Book', made up in 1674 and added to until 1784. In the second list are volumes of Collectanea made up by vice-chancellors Ashton (1702) and Sherlock (1714) on the duties of their office. Formularies and transcripts of various kinds make up the rest of the books listed in the catalogue. The most outstanding collection of transcripts is that of Robert Hare, clerk of the pells, presented to the university in 1587. As well as the beautifully engrossed and illuminated presentation set, bound in two volumes,[1] the vice-chancellor had the use of a plainer set of more handy size, bound in three volumes. The books and archives recorded in the two lists of 1657 and 1797 are now, almost without exception, in the university archives.

Also transferred annually on 1 October from outgoing to incoming proctors are the books of statutes, carried on chains as badges of their office. The university archives preserve the various volumes used for this purpose for the best part of six centuries, and the older books of statutes (see chapter 4) are of particular interest and value. The 'Old Proctor's Book', remaining from a pair probably written about 1390, contains two full-page illuminations of early fifteenth-century work.[2] The 'Senior Proctor's Book' and 'Junior Proctor's Book', which were used from about 1490 to 1785, with several rebindings, are a massive compendium in a variety of hands and styles. From about 1578 to 1683, the first leaves of each volume have been used as a sort of autograph album, each proctor writing his name, often followed by a classical tag or motto. From 1785 to 1882 a copy of the first printed edition of the statutes was carried by each proctor, as today a modern printed copy of the current statutes is concealed beneath the antique cover with its clasp and chain. With the 'Proctors' Books' in the archives is kept the 'Registrum Librorum' of 1473, in its original sheepskin binding, containing early catalogues of the archives, as well as of books and other valuables, from 1420 to 1620.

The early part of the sixteenth century, which was marked by many new developments in the spheres of university teaching and government, saw the creation of a different type of office, with tenure for life or until retirement. Some of the older offices changed to this tenure and were elevated in status; some new offices were created. During the fifteenth century the chancellor was often a non-resident magnate, and in 1514 Bishop Fisher (who had been reappointed at intervals since 1504) was elected chancellor for life. The office of high steward, recorded only sporadically in the fifteenth century, regularly follows the new pattern from about 1504, and this office was also held by a magnate and not by a resident master or doctor.

Also elevated, but not on such a grand scale as that of chancellor, was the ancient office of bedell. The medieval bedells had been non-graduates but, from

[1] Plate 3.   [2] Plate 1.

44

1490 usually, and from 1530 invariably, they were masters and were now dignified by the title of esquire bedell. From this period until 1863 there were normally three bedells, holding office for life or until retirement. For many years after life tenure had become customary, however, there lingered an echo of the older system in an annual ceremony, at which the bedells tendered up their staves (as badges of office) but had them returned.[1]

Closely associated with the office of bedell, from its inception by Grace in 1506, was the new office of registrary. All four of the sixteenth-century registraries were chosen from the ranks of the bedells and held office by the same tenure. It was not, however, thought necessary to vacate both offices simultaneously by retirement. From the appointment of James Tabor, who was not a bedell, in 1600, the offices were finally dissociated and vacancies were filled by open election in the usual way.

Following the same pattern of election and tenure were two other new offices of the sixteenth century, that of public orator, founded in 1522, and that of librarian, created in 1577, to replace, in part, the abolished office of the pre-Reformation university chaplain.[2]

The election to all these offices continued to preserve the ancient form, but under the Elizabethan statutes all nominations had first to be submitted to the heads for approval. The choice of the senate was further restricted by interpretations of the statutes in 1582 and 1663, by which the names of two candidates only were 'pricked' by the heads from the list of nominations and offered for election. The ballot at elections was open, the proctors taking the vote in the Regent House, and two scrutators in the non-Regent House.[3] Bundles of voting-papers for many contested elections of officers are preserved in the university archives. For the office of chancellor votes are extant from 1612, but for the others the series does not begin until the Commonwealth period. From 1780 to 1870 the polls were analysed and printed in pamphlet form. Those in the archives have been bound into small volumes. With these records of elections should be mentioned those for such professorships and teaching posts as were elective, similarly kept in the archives. The grant by royal charter in 1604 of the two university burgesses in

---

[1] Elizabethan Statutes xxxviii and xlv, and H. P. Stokes, *The Esquire Bedells of the University of Cambridge*, Cambridge Antiquarian Society 8° publication, no. xlv, chap. iv.

[2] H. P. Stokes, *The Chaplains and the Chapel of the University of Cambridge*, pp. 39 and 40.

[3] Elizabethan Statutes xxxv, xxxvi and xl, also Interpretations of the Statutes of 18 September 1582 and 9 October 1663.

parliament produced a notable series of electoral records, as the voting was usually heavier than for any other office. Until the reforms of 1857, elections of burgesses were conducted by the method used for all university elections to office and the polls similarly analysed. From 1857 to 1948, when the university vote was abolished, a system of secret ballot was operated, with single transferable vote from 1918.

University office in the sixteenth and seventeenth centuries was considered honourable and sought after, and it was well that the prestige-value of office-holding was high, for the pecuniary rewards were remarkably low by present standards. The orator, for instance, had to write all the university's Latin letters and speeches for a stipend of forty shillings per annum (soon doubled plus a few fees), but he was given precedence in university processions and ceremonies. The registrary had no regular fees while he was a bedell, and it was only as a result of Tabor's petition of 1623 that a fee of sixpence per head was charged at times of admission to degrees. The bedells were more fortunate in that their right of collecting fees from inceptors in arts had been established in the Middle Ages, and to these fees were added fines, rewards, bequests, and dinners, as well as a small stipend from 1570. In spite of some improvements as time went on, the pecuniary emoluments of most of the offices were not great, and continued to consist of a mixture of fees, small stipend, and occasional benefactions, until the reforms of 1856, when all were commuted for regular stipends.

The most notable records left by these officers in the university archives are, however, not the papers relating to the appointments, rights, and emoluments of office (which are bound into the series of C.U.R. guard-books under the names of the respective offices) but the volumes composed by various holders themselves, to aid their own memories and to instruct their successors. In many ways these volumes are similar to the books of statutes and collectanea written for the use of the vice-chancellor. Such, for instance, are the collections of registraries Tabor and Whinn, though containing more administrative detail and legal material. Of particular distinction and interest are the volumes of the earlier registraries, who were also bedells, John Mere and Matthew Stokys; for with the former began the custom of passing to his successor 'Those books that I have made concerning that offyce, that they remayn perpetually to the offyce'. Mere's contribution is known as the 'Liber Rerum Memorabilium' and is very miscellaneous in its contents. Mere also bequeathed, perhaps involuntarily, one of the diaries for which he is famous, as he wrote them on blank leaves of Grace Book A, when he had the custody of the books as esquire bedell.[1] Stokys' book is even more valuable than Mere's. Bound into the front is an early account of regulations for vespers, commencements and exercises in the various faculties, and the only existing pre-Reformation form for the commemoration of benefactors, dating from the first half of the reign of Henry VIII. The rest of the book, in Stokys' own distinctive hand, contains much of interest including lists of early officers of the university, which, if not absolutely accurate, are based on sources no longer available.[2]

The mid-sixteenth century also saw the creation of two permanent, but non-elective, offices to assist the chancellor in the exercise of his legal functions, those of commissary and university counsel. The former, acting as a deputy of the chancellor, was appointed by the chancellor's own letters patent.

There remain the offices held by patent or licence from the vice-chancellor, some of which were elective.[3] They were normally non-graduate offices, held by servants of the university, or tradespeople whose connection with the university entitled them to claim the status of 'privileged persons', a status which will be more fully discussed in relation to university jurisdiction (see chapters 10 and 11). They included such humbler posts as those of the university plumber, pewterer, and glazier; the university waits; the letter-carriers and pawnbroker who operated under licence from the vice-chancellor; the victuallers and vintners, also licensed by the vice-chancellor. A group of special interest were the university stationers, three of whom, under royal letters patent of 1534, rose to become university printers. Assisting the vice-chancellor in the exercise of his testamentary jurisdiction were the appraisers (also most confusingly called 'stationers', though not always stationers in the normal sense) and the assessor. Assisting in the survey of weights and measures and supervision of the market was the university gauger. The majority of these minor offices were abolished in 1856, when university jurisdiction was drastically curtailed and the status of 'privileged persons' abolished. They have left their traces in the university archives chiefly in odd licences and notices of appointment, or in vouchers for payment of bills due to them.

---

[1] *Grace Book* A, pp. 221–30 (fos. 52a–55b).

[2] 'Stokys' Book', fos. 13b–113a. Transcript of parts of 'Stokys' Book' in G. Peacock, *Observations on the Statutes*, Appendix A.

[3] Elizabethan Statutes XL, and H. Gunning, *The Ceremonies observed in the Senate House of the University of Cambridge* (Cambridge, 1828), pp. 249–50.

Special mention should, however, be made of the university marshal, the last of the ancient and honourable offices still held by a non-graduate. Patents of appointment for the marshal, issued by the vice-chancellor, are preserved in the archives from 1623. The mace he carries in university processions is that formerly borne by the yeoman bedell, another non-graduate officer, whose office was abolished in 1858.

10. RECORDS OF THE UNIVERSITY COURTS

The exercise of an independent jurisdiction in the regulation of its affairs and in the disciplining and protection of its members was, in the Middle Ages, a generally coveted privilege, to which many autonomous corporations aspired, and which constituted a source both of pride and of profit to the community which enjoyed it. Much of the early history of Cambridge university can be regarded as part of a long struggle for the establishment and extension of such a jurisdiction, which should be on the one hand free from the interference of the lay or common law system (represented by the royal justices and the local courts of the borough) and on the other hand independent of the higher ecclesiastical courts, of which the chancellor's court had originally been a humble offshoot. The university would not of itself have been sufficiently wealthy or powerful to achieve such a position had it not been fortunate enough to enjoy the support and patronage of the crown and of the pope, shown in the long series of royal and episcopal charters (chapter 4). By their aid, however, what was at first a very necessary protection for the university in hostile surroundings, and later primarily an affair of honour, was operating in the later medieval and Tudor periods as a flourishing system of courts, based on the privileged jurisdiction of the chancellor.

By the time of Elizabeth I, the university had acquired a highly privileged jurisdiction. By her letters patent of 26 April 1561, the queen declared the university court to be a court of record, and confirmed Richard II's grant to it of jurisdiction over civil proceedings in which title to land was not concerned, and over criminal proceedings for all offences below the grade of felonies and mayhems, whenever one of the parties to the proceedings enjoyed the privilege of the university. At the same time, she provided a higher criminal jurisdiction by granting that whenever any person enjoying the privilege of the university should be accused by a 'layman', at the assizes or quarter-sessions, of having committed treason or felony or mayhem in the town or county of Cambridge, the university might claim the prisoner. He would then be tried by its high steward (Senescallus Cancellarii) and according to the common law. In such cases, a jury would be empanelled, half of them being members of the university. In 1571, by the Act for the Incorporation of the Universities (13 Eliz. I, c. 29), her letters patent of 1561, and all other letters patent granted by any of her predecessors to either of the universities, were declared to be as of full legal effect 'as if the same letters-patent were recited verbatim in this present Act of Parliament'. These enactments placed beyond challenge the authority of the university court and the power of the chancellor to employ a civil law procedure. Almost simultaneously, a room on the east side of the Schools Quadrangle was fitted up[1] as a consistory court for the use of the vice-chancellor, who by this time presided in the chancellor's court.

In 1600/1, as we find from a description of the university submitted by the registrary Tabor to Sir Robert Cecil on his becoming chancellor, the consistory court sat weekly in term time to administer justice.[2] Its procedure had been from medieval times (as was also that of the commissary's court) similar to that of the other spiritual courts; use of canon and civil law, and competence to deal with ecclesiastical persons and causes. (The chancellor had originally possessed the power of excommunication, which he exercised rather unfairly in quarrels with the mayor; but this was renounced in temporal causes in 1534.) Even after the Reformation, the procedure, the use of civil law, and much of the jurisdiction remained, while the vice-chancellor retained quasi-episcopal powers such as that of licensing preachers or giving dispensations for eating flesh in Lent. Documents illustrating these powers are extant in the archives. Disciplinary and some moral causes were dealt with by the vice-chancellor's court, and there also fell to it the unenviable task of enforcing the various religious settlements. The essentially

---

[1] Willis and Clark, *Architectural History*, vol. III, p. 22.
[2] *The Historical Register of the University of Cambridge*, ed. J. R. Tanner, p. 65.

ecclesiastical character of the court was shown by its having power to grant probate of the wills of resident members of the university, and other 'privileged' persons. (For a more detailed description of the classes of 'privileged' persons, see chapter 11.)

The vice-chancellor's court could suspend from degrees and could imprison but, by a university statute of 1569, any sentence of imprisonment passed upon a doctor, or a sentence of expulsion passed upon anyone, was ineffectual unless assented to by the majority of the heads of colleges. From this court there lay an appeal to the university itself, which would be heard by delegates elected by the senate (as laid down by statute XLVIII of 1570), as in the well known case of Mr Frend in 1793. Finally, there could be an appeal to the king in council.

In the inferior court over which the commissary presided, on the other hand, no case could be dealt with in which anyone of so high a degree as that of a master of arts was concerned. From it an appeal lay to the chancellor's court, and thence to the university delegates.

The chief executive officials of these courts, after the vice-chancellor and his commissary, were the proctors, whose duties included acting as university police and enforcing discipline among junior members of the university. They were assisted by the taxors, the gaugers, and others. An assessor and four appraisers were appointed chiefly to assist the vice-chancellor in the exercise of his testamentary jurisdiction. The registrary was clerk of the courts.

The high steward seems not to have tried any case for 'many years', before 1798, and in 1852 the university commissioners found that the high steward's jurisdiction had 'become in practice a merely nominal power', except in his Court Leet for superintending weights and measures.

The numerous Act Books of the vice-chancellor's court, dating from 1552 to 1861, Books of Depositions, 1591 to 1675, and 'Exhibita' files, 1559 to 1697, which are in the university archives, testify to the court's great activity over a long period, and provide much valuable material for the study of social and economic history, especially for the sixteenth and seventeenth centuries. This is equally true of the records of the commissary's court, which sat both in the university and in Midsummer and Sturbridge fairs. There are Act Books, dating from 1580 to 1746, Books of Depositions, 1580 to 1640, 'Exhibita' files, 1580 to 1692, and the 'Acta' at Sturbridge fair, 1562 to 1835.

In March 1956, the earliest and most important series of the records of the vice-chancellor's court, the testamentary records, were returned to the university archives. They had been in the District Probate Registry at Peterborough for more than ninety years.[1] These comprise some 1550 original wills proved between about 1540 and 1765, five volumes of registers of wills dating from 1501 to 1765, as well as about 1300 inventories of the testators' possessions dating from 1498 to 1761, University Administration Bonds, 1534–1746, and other records relating to senior members of the university, and to certain other 'privileged persons'. It is also important to note here the many interesting signatures of outstanding figures of the university who witnessed the wills. These probate records are arranged chronologically at present, and it should perhaps be mentioned here that the *Calendar of Wills proved in Vice-Chancellor's Court at Cambridge, 1501–1765*, does not include the inventories. Of particular interest to bibliographers are those inventories containing lists of books.[2] There are approximately 167 such lists in the Cambridge inventories, a larger number than Oxford possesses. These book-lists are an invaluable source of information about reading habits at the time of the English Renaissance, showing as they do the books actually in possession of, and presumably read by, those connected with the university. The lists from the early sixteenth century show a dominating concern with theology, which gives way, slowly after the mid-century, to a much greater interest in classical literature.

In 1828 the act of parliament of 9 Geo. IV, c. 31 conferred upon Justices of the Peace sitting in petty sessions a summary jurisdiction over cases of assault; and the act contained no reservation of the university's hitherto exclusive jurisdiction over cases in which its members were concerned. Already, however, the vice-chancellor's court seems to have found its business greatly diminished. While civil law procedure was felt to give a real benefit and privilege, as was the case in the sixteenth and early seventeenth centuries, it was difficult to limit the numbers of persons who pressed their claims to be heard in the university courts. During the eighteenth century, however, when, on more than one occasion, the university failed to make good its claims and civil law procedure was felt to be anachronistic, claims of cognizance more or less died out. The last was made in 1844 and disallowed.[3] In 1852 the commissioners reported that the court was already

[1] C. J. B. Gaskoin, 'The University Wills at Peterborough', *Camb. Ant. Soc. Proc.* vol. x (O.S.), no. XLIV (pp. 314–16).   [2] Plate 11.

[3] Helen M. Cam, 'The City of Cambridge', *Victoria County History of Cambridgeshire*, vol. III, p. 83. Also C. H. Cooper, *Annals of Cambridge*, vol. IV (1852 edn.), p. 667, and D. A. Winstanley, *Unreformed Cambridge*, p. 31.

obsolete except in cases of discommuning or of a university man's breach of discipline. Thus the way was easy for the Cambridge Award Act of 1856, to provide (S. 18) that 'the right of the University, or any officer thereof to claim conusance of any action or criminal proceeding, wherein any person who is not a member of the University shall be a party, shall cease and determine'.

The statutes of 1858 laid down that in civil causes that fell within the scope of academical jurisdiction the Cambridge chancellor's powers might be exercised by the commissary, unless a master of arts or one of higher degree was one of the litigants; but in that case the chancellor or vice-chancellor must sit. The composition of this court, formerly called the 'Sex Viri', was, by an amendment of statute B, approved by the king in council on 2 February 1937, changed to the 'Septemviri'. Five members of the court constitute a quorum. Three of these members are appointed each year at a congregation and hold office for two years.

Persons *in statu pupillari*, that is to say, junior members of the university, are subject to the Court of Discipline and the proctors. The Court of Discipline, which consists of the vice-chancellor and six heads of colleges, has jurisdiction over any person *in statu pupillari* who is charged with any offence against the discipline of the university or with acting in a manner discreditable to the university. Proceedings of this court and also that of the 'Septemviri' are recorded by the registrary in volumes which remain in his custody. These include a composite volume entitled 'Appointments of Deputies' and 'Cases tried by Sex Viri' which appear to cover the dates 1862–1921 and 1864–1938 respectively, a volume called 'Acta Curiae 1887' and also entitled 'Court of Discipline', 1887–1946, and a volume entitled 'Orders of the Vice-Chancellor and Heads' (which also includes some of the later proceedings of the Court of Discipline), 1899–1955. (There is an overlap with volumes 2 and 3.)

Regulations governing the behaviour of persons *in statu pupillari* are given in detail in the edicts to be found in the current *Statutes and Ordinances of the University of Cambridge*, and in a handbook called *A Compendium of University Regulations*. Breaches of discipline are usually dealt with by the proctors or their deputies, the pro-proctors, unless the matter is a serious one, in which case it is referred to the Court of Discipline. The proctors keep records of their own activities, and the volumes containing them are duly handed on to their successors.

11. RECORDS OF UNIVERSITY JURISDICTION IN THE TOWN OF CAMBRIDGE

Although the university was an autonomous and privileged corporation, keeping, as far as possible, its own functions and members within its own jurisdiction, it could not be entirely independent of another ancient and privileged corporation on its doorstep, the borough of Cambridge. In fact, the borough could claim the greater antiquity, in that its earliest extant charter, that of 1207, antedates the oldest in the university archives by almost sixty years.[1]

In the medieval university, as now, large numbers of scholars lodged in the town and, from its earliest days, the university was concerned to protect its members against extortionate rents, and against poor quality and high prices of provisions, as well as from assault by hostile townsfolk. In cases of breaches of the peace committed by the scholars themselves, which were by no means uncommon among these turbulent and unruly clerks, the university was at pains to keep its offending members from the jurisdiction of the royal justices in eyre and from the cognizance of the borough courts. Even from the sixteenth century, when most members of the university lived in colleges, both collegians and townsfolk walked the same streets, drank the same water and were supplied from the same markets. As the university pressed its claims to protect and control its members in every aspect of their lives, it was inevitable that it should come to interfere largely in the concerns of town and townsmen, and that friction should occur. The story of how that friction produced a state comparable at times to petty warfare between the two communities for a great part of their history, until its causes were removed by the Cambridge Award Act of 1856, has been admirably and fully described in the most recent volume of the *Victoria County History*.[2] Here it is sufficient to mention points of conflict, agreements, and extensions of the university privilege, only in so far as they have been productive of records in the university archives.

Various attempts were made by the crown in the thirteenth century to establish

---

[1] F. W. Maitland and M. Bateson, *Cambridge Borough Charters*, p. 6 and frontispiece.

[2] Helen M. Cam, 'The City of Cambridge: Town and Gown', *Victoria County History of Cambridgeshire*, vol. III, pp. 76–86.

joint responsibility between town and university in dealing with possible causes of friction. Some of the earliest documents relating to the university, the recorded writ of 1231 and the earliest extant charter of 1266, provide for the assessment, by two officials each of the university and borough, of the rents of scholars' houses. Under a charter of 1268, while the responsibility for keeping the peace rested primarily with the town, the chancellor of the university could claim the person of a clerk who attacked a layman. The chancellor was required to assist the mayor in the Assize of Bread.[1] Two years later, following the important arbitration made by the Lord Edward, the 'Magna Congregatio' or 'Black Assembly' was established, on which representatives of university and borough took an oath to preserve the peace.[2] This annual ceremony has left no early records in the university archives, although it is illustrated by a crude sketch in Hare's transcripts (c. 1590) and was described by Mere and later by Gunning. It is clear that by Mere's day the taking of the oath was considered to mark the university's precedence over the town, and as such was bitterly resented.[3] Quarrels over precedency in public ceremonies reached their peak in the debate before the queen's commissioners in 1601 and the case in council of 1612 (both of which have left papers in the archives), but from 1544 to 1788 the function and records of the Black Leet were merged with those of the Paving Leet. A small volume entitled 'Magna Congregatio and Black Leet, 1817–1855' covers the period from the revival of the ceremony by a tactless vice-chancellor to its final extinction.

In spite of the royal attempt at mediation, causes of friction remained and increased. The settlement of 1268 and 1270 was undermined, both by the early exhibited tendency of the university officials to assume superiority over those of the town, and, even more, by the growth of the jurisdiction of the university courts at the expense of those of the borough. Further royal charters of 14 February and 3 June 1317 extended the chancellor's jurisdiction over a great variety of personal actions between clerks and laymen, and over more classes of cases of injury inflicted by clerks on laymen and vice versa. In 1337 complaint was made by the burgesses to the king that, as a result of these grants, laymen injuring clerks were punished, while aggressive clerks were liberated; and that scholars purchased

[1] C. H. Cooper, *Annals of Cambridge*, vol. 1 (1842 edn.), pp. 46 and 51.
[2] Document no. 3 (Luard's list). The text of this arbitration is best preserved in the university archives in document no. 7*, the Inspeximus of Edward I, 1291/2 (plate 12).
[3] Mere's Diary, *Grace Book* A, p. 225 (fo. 53a).

debts and contracts and sued for them in the chancellor's court.[1] The charter of 14 February 1317 also offended in that it prescribed a ceremony in which the mayor and bailiffs, on taking office, had to swear to maintain the privileges of the university. Mounting ill-feeling between the town and the university during the fourteenth century came to a head in the great riots of 1381. The crown, making inquiry into the matter, visited the town with severe royal displeasure (see chapter 1).

ASSIZE OF BREAD, LICENSING, WEIGHTS AND MEASURES

By royal charter of 17 February 5 Ric. II, for the payment of an annual subsidy of £10 to the exchequer, the university received sole custody of the assize of bread, wine and ale, survey of weights and measures, and cognizance of trading in victuals in the town and suburbs of Cambridge, with all profits of justice arising therefrom, as fully and freely as the mayor and corporation of the borough had formerly enjoyed them. The final clause of the charter contained the bitterest pill the latter had to swallow: '...mandamus, quod in praemissis...faciendis Cancellario... vel eius...Commissario auxilientur, pareant humiliter, et intendant, prout decet.' In the following year the survey of weights and measures at Sturbridge fair was confirmed to the university by letters patent.[2]

This extremely important charter was the basis of the university's control of the Cambridge market and of all trading in victuals for a considerable distance round the town, together with the power of issuing licences for vintners, victuallers, and keepers of ale-houses. It lasted until the act following the award of Sir John Patteson in 1856, and in one respect, the issuing of wine licences, the privilege remains to this day. It proved a profitable source of revenue to the university, a deep-seated cause of resentment on the part of the town. It also added considerably to the executive duties of the proctors and their assistants, the taxors, the gauger, and the clerk of the market, with their servants. The more important ceremonies connected with these privileges were the Proclamation of the Markets in October, the Proclamation of the Fairs on 23 June and 18 September, and the

---

[1] C. H. Cooper, *Annals of Cambridge*, vol. 1 (1842 edn.), p. 90.
[2] George Dyer, *The Privileges of the University of Cambridge* (London, 1824), vol. 1, pp. 82–4.

Survey of Weights and Measures soon after Easter. The form in which they were made at the end of the eighteenth century has been described by Gunning.[1]

From 1382 the university held a Court Leet, under the presidency of the high steward or his deputy, for the exercise of the jurisdiction acquired by this privilege. The series of Leet Rolls preserved in the university archives runs, with some gaps, for four hundred years from 1383.[2] The later Leet Rolls are reduced to a list of Cambridge public houses fined for use of unsealed measures or for allowing unlawful games, like nine-pins. These proctors' leets are quite distinct from the Black Leet and Paving Leet, held conjointly with the borough. While simple cases of breaches of regulations were dealt with by fines at the Proctors' Leet, more serious cases were brought into the university's other courts, the commissary's court being used for such cases arising at the fairs.

The area in which the university's jurisdiction was exercised both with regard to privileges of trading and to supervision of morals was extended in the seventeenth century beyond what could reasonably be called the suburbs of Cambridge. The charter of James I of 1605 defined the area as one mile beyond the most outward buildings of the town in every direction, and for the prohibition of idle games and diversions decreed a five-mile limit. The university archives contain certificates from the seventeenth century, issued by the vice-chancellor, known as Five Mile Certificates, stating that the village in question—even as far away as Wimpole—was within the 'five-mile limit' and should come within the privilege.

With the exception of the Leet Rolls, already mentioned, records relating to the university's supervision of trade, licensing, and victualling are not preserved earlier than the mid-sixteenth century, possibly because there was no central repository for them before the construction of the register office. Books of the Assize of Bread run from 1596 to 1836, and records relating to licensing of victuallers from 1596 to 1856. Vintner's licences and related documents are preserved from a little earlier, the first surviving licence being that granted by John Yonge, V.C., to Simon Watson, bookbinder and stationer, to be vintner, on 10 November 1553.[3] Ale-house licences, called in periodically for renewal (at a fee), are preserved from 1616 to 1836. In addition there are books of regula-

[1] H. Gunning, *The Ceremonies of the University of Cambridge*, pp. 41, 118, and 129.
[2] *Ibid.* p. 102. Also C.U.R. 17 (Court Leets, 1383–1615) and Leet Rolls 1600–1782 in boxes.
[3] C. P. Hall, 'Two Licences granted to Cambridge Stationers'. *Trans. of the Camb. Bibliog. Socy.* vol. I (1953), pp. 443–4.

tions for the fair and the markets, with a quantity of miscellaneous papers, for the later sixteenth and early seventeenth centuries. Two quaint pictures from the reign of Elizabeth I have descended to us with the written records. A large wooden tablet presented by Matthew Stokys, depicting the duties of the clerk of the market, hangs in the registry. The smaller sketch in Hare's transcripts illustrating the Survey of weights and measures, shows the proctors, taxors, and gauger testing weights by the standards and the destruction of false measures.[1] A standard bushel measure of 1641, used for this survey, has long stood in the registry office.

The standard measures held by the university were in their turn subject to inspection by the exchequer from at least Tudor times. Documents relating to the taxors in the university archives include records of a number of such checks between 1564 and 1826, when new standards were received, listed, and described.[2] These documents were put to effective use in 1952. There was reason to believe that other ancient weights and measures, which had formerly stood in the registry with the standard bushel, and whose provenance had been lost, had been deposited first in the Cambridge Museum of Archaeology and Ethnology, and subsequently in the Science Museum at South Kensington. From the documents in the university archives, it was possible to establish the identity of the measures, so that they were returned to the university and are now permanently on view in the Regent House. The standards still in use in 1856, when the university's right to survey was abolished, also have an interesting story attached to them. By Grace of October 1856 the university agreed to place its standards on indefinite loan to the borough corporation, and a bond in £400 was signed to this effect. A century later, on 22 October 1956, this bond was formally cancelled at a ceremony in the Guildhall, and the city corporation received in perpetuity the possession of the standards, which are kept in the custody of the city inspector of weights and measures.[3]

PRIVILEGED PERSONS

The protection which the university claimed to exercise over its own members had early been extended to certain classes of tradesmen who served the needs of learning: writers, stationers, bookbinders and illuminators, 'whose trespasses were justiciable by the Chancellor'. In the year following the great 'Charter of Assize

---

[1] Plate 13.   [2] C.U.R. 35 (Taxors).   [3] Some are now in the Cambridge Folk Museum.

and Assay', a further grant from the crown of 10 December 1383 redefined, to the university's advantage, the limits of the chancellor's jurisdiction in cases where 'a master, scholar, scholar's servant or common minister of the University be a party'.[1] The university's privilege was thus established over servants of the university, as well as over those of individual masters and scholars, and these persons were generally known as 'scholar's servants' or 'privileged persons'. The matter of 'privileged persons' rankled with the town, as they enjoyed exemption from the routine duties and common charge of the borough, as well as freedom from the borough courts. Wills of 'privileged persons', like those of members of the university, were proved in the vice-chancellor's court and so entered, from the inception of the first Register of Wills in 1501 (see chapter 2).

In the important award between the university and the town, made at the instance of the Lady Margaret on 11 July 1502, the numbers of privileged persons were again increased by the provision

that all Bedells of the University, & all Manciples, Cooks, Buttlers, & Launderers of every College and Hall; also, all Apothecarys, Stationers, Lymners, Scriveners, Parchment Makers, Bookbinders, Physitians, Surgeons & Barbers in the said University...shall have the Privilege of Scholars Servant, as long as they use any such Occupation.[2]

To both the copy of the award and of the composition confirming it of 12 May 1503, in the university archives, a schedule of persons in the privilege is appended, about seventy names in all.[3] In 1589 the privilege was again extended to some further categories of college and university servants, ranging from the keeper of the university library to the husbands of married college laundresses. Of more moment was the provision that the families and household servants of all married graduates living in the town should also be included. In 1596 complaint was made that about eleven score persons of graduate families, dwelling in the town and making their living by trade, were consequently escaping the burdens that fell on the other townsmen.[4] At this time the number of persons claiming and enjoying privileged status was probably at its greatest extent.

An oath was required of all persons entering the privilege and the normal form of 'Oath of Scholar's Servants' is inscribed in the first Matriculation Register of

---

[1] George Dyer, *Privileges*, vol. I, pp. 86–8; also J. P. C. Roach, 'The University of Cambridge', *Victoria County History of Cambridgeshire*, vol. III, p. 155.

[2] George Dyer, *Privileges*, vol. I, pp. 97–8.   [3] Documents nos. 141–3 (Luard's list).

[4] C. H. Cooper, *Annals of Cambridge*, vol. II (1843 edn.), p. 561; also MS. letters of Dr Jegon.

1544. But at Cambridge, unlike Oxford, names of 'privileged persons' ceased to be entered in the Matriculation Register after the first few years. They were kept in separate lists, which have been bound together for the years 1524–1720.[1] For a very short period (1755–60) there was an attempt to keep a separate register of privileged persons in the back of the Matriculation Register. By this time the numbers had declined considerably and were almost entirely confined to university and college servants. The status of 'privileged persons' was finally abolished by the Cambridge Award Act of 1856.

POLICE AND GAOL

The award of 1502–3 touched on another long-standing cause of dispute between the university and the town in the provision 'that the Keepers of the Town Prisons shall keep such Prisoners, as are committed by the Chancellor in convenient & secure Places; & shall take no Fees of a privileged Person...'.[2] The university had no right to a gaol of its own and in early days, following royal letters of 1242 (confirmed in 1294) directed to the sheriff of Cambridge, the chancellor could give his mandate for the imprisonment in the castle of contumacious clerks and others under the chancellor's jurisdiction.[3] The town took exception to the imprisonment of townsmen outside the boundaries of the borough, and the university claimed the right to use the tolbooth, or town prison, for the chancellor's prisoners. Disputes arose when the town's officials failed to obey the chancellor's mandate in committing or releasing prisoners, and over fees. It was not until 1603 that James I granted by charter to the university the right to have its own gaol. In 1628 a House of Correction was built for the joint use of university and town under Hobson's Charity Trust, a House which was thus described in the mid-eighteenth century:

The Bridewell (called by the inhabitants the Spinning House) is pleasantly situated near the fields at the south end of the parish of Great St Andrew's, and is chiefly used for the confinement of such lewd women as the Proctors apprehend..., though sometimes the Corporation send small offenders thither, and the crier of the town is often there to discipline the ladies of pleasure with his whip.[4]

[1] C.U.R. 36.2 (Privileged Persons and Claims of Cognizance). See also C.U.R. 36.1 (Ship Money and Lists of Privileged Persons). [2] George Dyer, *Privileges*, vol. I, p. 99.
[3] C. H. Cooper, *Annals of Cambridge*, vol. I (1842 edn.), p. 44; also document no. 11 (Luard's list).
[4] Edmund Carter, *The History of the County of Cambridge* (London, 1819 edn.), p. 19.

After the building of the new town gaol in 1829 the Spinning House remained the vice-chancellor's prison and was in practice used solely for one class of prisoner, the 'lewd women' mentioned above.

The proctors, in the exercise of their discipline over the manners and morals of members of the university, had anciently acquired the right of searching for and apprehending such women. This right was specifically confirmed to them in several royal grants, sometimes in connection with the right or duty of inquiring into other kinds of street nuisances as in the 'Carta de mundatione viarum et de meretricibus banniendis', of 12 April 1459.[1] These rights of presentment and arrest, together with their rights to search for bad flesh and fish, forestallers and regrators, and other persons who contravened trading provisions, and with such joint responsibility as the university had with the town in keeping the peace, made the proctors and their servants (the 'bulldogs') in effect a police force, acting concurrently with and independently from the town police. The two rival police forces could in emergency (as in the case of the 1549 riots against enclosure) act together, but fell out upon more than one occasion, most notably in 1559, when a recommendation that they should join together for the night watches brought a free fight between them at the fair.[2]

After 1788, matters of public amenities were the business of the Improvement Commissioners, and control of trade was no longer as rigorously exercised (outside the ale-houses) as formerly, but the proctors continued actively to patrol the streets. In 1833 they were stated to be considerably more efficient than the town watchmen (this was before the setting up of the Borough Watch Committee in 1835) and complaints were made of the state of the town in the Long Vacation.[3] It was probably for this reason that the Cambridge Award Act of 1856 retained the proctorial system and set up a joint Watch Committee, and at the time of the lawsuit Kemp v. Neville of 1860–1,[4] when a good deal of hostility was exhibited against the proctors and the Spinning House, a memorial was signed by the mayor and many residents of Cambridge in favour of the continuance of the proctorial system of policing. Feelings of resentment against the very existence of a prerogative jurisdiction and of a prison for those whom the vice-chancellor detained

[1] Document no. 124 (Luard's list).
[2] C. H. Cooper, *Annals of Cambridge*, vol. II (1843 edn.), p. 155.
[3] Helen M. Cam, 'The City of Cambridge', *Victoria County History of Cambridgeshire*, vol. III, p. 78.
[4] C.U.R. 41.3. Proctorial Suit (Kemp v. Neville).

outside the normal course of the common law continued to grow. With the cases of Jane Elsden and Daisy Hopkins in 1891, the matter came to a head in a burst of public indignation. Finally, after conferences between the two authorities, the Cambridge University and Corporation Act of 1894 was promoted, providing for concurrent action by proctors and town police in arresting loose women and abolishing the vice-chancellor's jurisdiction over them. The vice-chancellor's power to license theatres (another relic of his jurisdiction over morals) was abolished by the same act.

The minutes of the University Improvement Syndicate (for improving the town and the university) of 1824–30, and the report of the syndicate respecting the borough police and Cambridge Improvement Act of 1851 are kept in the university archives, with very full documentation of the cases of 1860 and 1891 mentioned above. Books of Spinning House Committals, with the proctors' notes on individuals arrested (for example, 'very violent, had to be fetched in a cab'), run from 1823 to 1894. A number of papers, relating to the Hobson's Charity Trust and to the internal administration of the Spinning House in the nineteenth century, give a detailed picture of an experiment in social reform which does not seem to have been entirely successful. Perhaps most interesting are the Spinning House Regulations, in the copy certified by Lord Palmerston as Home Secretary on 21 February 1854, and the Dietary.[1]

PUBLIC HEALTH AND AMENITIES, CHARITIES

Although the university maintained that supervision and control of the food supply of Cambridge was necessary to preserve the health and well-being of its members, it claimed no such independent jurisdiction with regard to the water supply, cleansing of sewers and streets, and disposal of refuse. These matters remained throughout the Middle Ages the responsibility of the town, as laid down in the royal order of 1268, and the university's part was confined to making com-

---

[1] *Report of the Commissioners for Inquiring into Charities, 1838*; H. P. Stokes, *Outside the Barnwell Gate*, Cambridge Antiquarian Society 8° publications, no. XLVII, pp. 33–6; and H. P. Stokes, 'Cambridge Parish Workhouses', *Camb. Ant. Soc. Proc.* vol. XV (O.S.), no. LIX, pp. 87–94. There is a photograph of the Spinning House (*c.* 1896) in the chapter on the city of Cambridge in the *Victoria County History of Cambridgeshire*, vol. III (plate opp. p. 77).

plaints when the mayor failed to perform his duties (as happened frequently).[1] In 1390 the vice-chancellor was ordered to act with the mayor in enforcing the recent statute of Cambridge[2] of 1388 against 'them which cause corruptions near a city or great town to corrupt the air'. In 1459 the vice-chancellor was empowered to inquire into nuisances at the university leet and to fine offenders, and the award of 1502-3 extended his authority to act upon any presentment of nuisance after six weeks, if the mayor failed to do so. By act of parliament of 1544, a Paving Leet was set up, to be held jointly by mayor and vice-chancellor, for enforcing the statutory responsibility now placed upon each householder for paving the roadway in front of his house, and for dealing with nuisances. The Paving Leet remained the sanitary authority in Cambridge for nearly two and a half centuries. Its meetings were combined with those of the Black Leet and joint records were kept.

The Paving Leet justified its existence chiefly as machinery for collecting fines and the town remained as insanitary as before. Epidemics of various kinds were frequent and from the mid-sixteenth to the mid-seventeenth centuries the town suffered serious visitations of the plague. Because the worst outbreaks usually took place in the Long Vacation, and the Long Vacation was more than once specially lengthened when severe sickness was prevalent, the members of the university managed to avoid infection more successfully than the townsfolk. But realising that plague and other infectious diseases knew no 'privileged persons' the vice-chancellor made common cause with the mayor in the face of common danger. Emergency orders were issued by their joint authority, the vice-chancellor's name appearing first, and a number of such orders are preserved in the university archives. One, dated 30 August 1563, provides for the lighting of street fires and more thorough cleansing of streets. Another of 1570 forbids the entry of persons from Yarmouth into the town, because there is plague in the former place. For the severe outbreaks of 1625, 1630, and 1665-6, detailed documents are preserved showing the preventive measures taken, bills of mortality, and attempts to relieve sufferers and survivors. Most strenuous in his endeavours to combat the plague in 1630 was vice-chancellor Dr Butts, master of Corpus, who shortly afterwards took his own life. The very complete set of mortality bills in the archives for the

---

[1] Helen Cam, 'The City of Cambridge: Public Health', *Victoria County History of Cambridgeshire*, vol. III, pp. 101-6.

[2] Document no. 74 (Luard's list); also C. H. Cooper, *Annals of Cambridge*, vol. I (1842 edn.), p. 134.

last extensive visitation of the plague in 1665–6 has been analysed and described.[1] An excellent lecture by Dr R. Williamson, describing the state of public health in medieval and Tudor Cambridge and in particular the outbreaks of plague, from the point of view of a medical practitioner, and incorporating material transcribed from the university archives, has also been published.[2]

A letter to Lord Burghley, the chancellor of the university, from Dr Perne, vice-chancellor and master of Peterhouse, in 1574, conjectures that, after 'our synnes', the most notable cause of the plague is the corruption of the King's Ditch. This open sewer, which joined the river at two points to complete the encirclement of the centre of the town, had caused trouble from the early Middle Ages, because of the insufficient flow of water in a flat area to keep it scoured. Dr Perne suggested that an additional pure water supply should be brought from Shelford, through Trumpington, to the town. It was not until thirty years later that the project was carried out, in the cutting of the 'New River' or 'Hobson's Brook', agreed to and subscribed to by members of university and town alike. The university part of the indenture of 1610 with Thomas Chaplyn, lord of the manor of Trumpington, for the lease of the route of the new watercourse is in the university archives.[3] There is also preserved a quantity of other material relating to drains, sewers and commons, matters closely interconnected in low-lying places subject to flooding, and of equal concern to university and town. Three volumes of papers run from c. 1618 to 1827.[4]

Cambridge was also concerned with some of the larger projects for fen drainage attempted in the early seventeenth century, and in the archives there are the royal Commissions of Sewers of 1618 and 1631, Orders for Sewers, and two volumes of Books of Sewers relating to the work of these commissioners of 1618. The fact that registrary Tabor was also clerk of the sewers probably accounts for their preservation.[5] The problem of Cambridge's water-supply was happily solved in the mid-nineteenth century, following the University and Town Waterworks Act of 1853,

[1] C.U.R. 54 and 54.2 (Plague); also C. P. Murrell, 'The Plague in Cambridge', *The Cambridge Review*, vol. LXII (1951), pp. 375–6 and 403–6.

[2] R. Williamson, 'The Plague in Cambridge', *Medical History*, vol. I, no. I (1957), pp. 51–64.

[3] W. D. Bushell, *Hobson's Conduit: The New River at Cambridge commonly called Hobson's River* (Cambridge, 1938).

[4] C.U.R. 3.1, 3.2 and 3.3 (Commons, Drains, Sewers, Conduit, etc.).

[5] Commissions of Sewers, nos. L, 79–89, and L. E. Harris, *Vermuyden and the Fens* (London, 1953), chapter VII.

by the foundation in 1855 of the University and Town Waterworks Company. For more than a century, this jointly owned company has brought good water from the Fulbourn area and efficient service to university and town. By the Cam Navigation Act of 1851, the powers of the conservators of the river Cam, composed of representatives appointed by the university, the county and the borough, were revised and extended. Copies of both these acts were deposited in the university archives.

Another sphere in which the co-operation of university and town, rather than their enmity, brought beneficial results, is that of charities and institutions of public benefit. The most notable example is perhaps Addenbrooke's Hospital. Among the jointly administered charities which have left their records in the university archives are those of Stokys' Alms Houses, Wray's Charity, Storey's Charity, and Worts' Endowment (particularly that part of it relating to Worts' Causeway). The university contributed to the relief of the poor of Cambridge, and to various appeals for charitable objects. The university archives preserve papers of the later seventeenth century relating to poor relief and detailed accounts of a special petition in aid of sufferers from a fire at Grantchester in February 1693/4, to which university and colleges gave donations.[1]

In 1788 a new statutory body, known as the Improvement Commissioners, representing the university, corporation, and parishes of Cambridge, took over from the negligent Paving Leet the responsibility of paving and lighting the town. To that end it had authority to levy a general rate. Books of orders and accounts of the Improvement Commissioners in the university archives run from 1788 to 1890. Receipts of the university contribution to the Poor Rate are kept from 1826 to 1856. Under the Cambridge Award Act of 1856, new arrangements were made for rating the university and colleges. Valuations of the rateable property of the university and colleges, with detailed plans, are preserved for 1860 and 1879. In 1889, under the Cambridge Corporation Act, the borough took over the functions of the Improvement Commissioners, and the university was content to leave matters of public amenity to the new borough council, on which it had representation.

[1] C.U.R. 19 (Miscellanea), no. 20.

1. Old Proctor's Book, *c.* 1390, fo. 6*a*. Illumination of St Christopher
(probably fifteenth-century work). (See pp. 27 and 44.)

2. Registrum Librorum, fo. 9 a. Inventory of the University Archives 1420 compiled by William Rysley. (See p. 5.)

3. Transcripts of the privileges of the university presented by Robert Hare, 1587, vol. I, fo. 17. (See pp. 16 and 44.)

4. Order of Service for the Commemoration of Benefactors, the first to be drawn up after the Reformation; authorised by the senate, February 1640/1, pp. 6 and 7. (See pp. 18 and 39.)

5. Bull of Pope Eugenius IV, 18 September 1433, confirming the exemption of the university from archiepiscopal and episcopal jurisdiction. (See p. 25.)

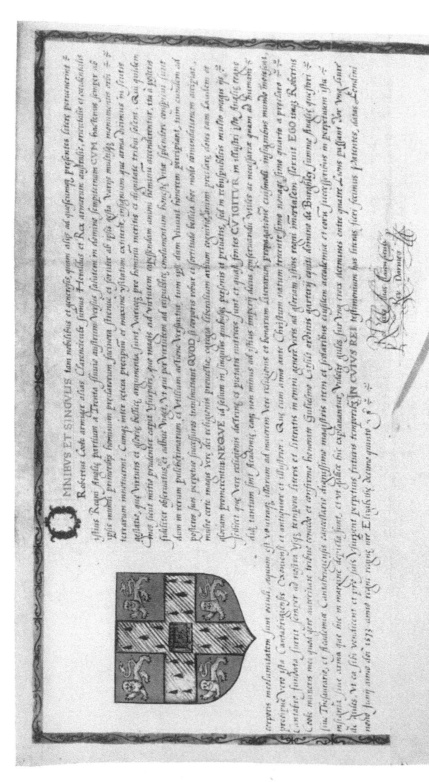

6. Grant of Arms to the university, 9 June 1573. (See p. 26n.)

7. Letters patent for grant of arms of the first five regius professors, 8 November 1590. (See p. 26n.)

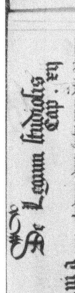

8 Statutes of 1570 given to the university by Queen Elizabeth I, fos. 2b and 4a. (See pp. 27 and 65.)

9. Proctor's Indenture, 1363, accounting for the contents of the Chest (from C.U.R. 1. 2, no. 1*a*).
The earliest surviving university account. (See pp. 1 and 34.)

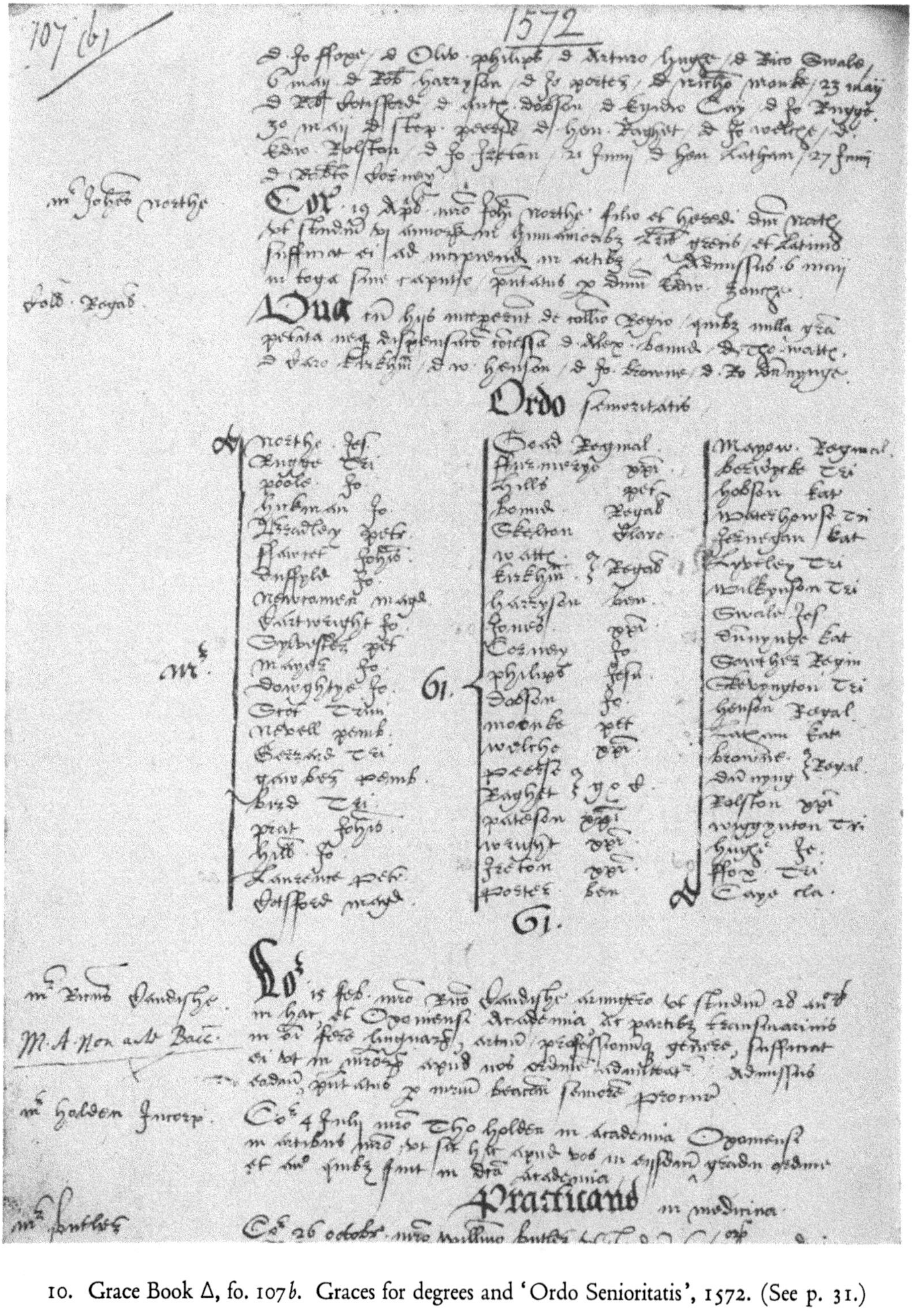
107 (b)

1572

Ordo senioritatis

Practicans in medicina

10. Grace Book Δ, fo. 107*b*. Graces for degrees and 'Ordo Senioritatis', 1572. (See p. 31.)

11. Inventory of goods and chattels of Dr Andrew Perne, master of Peterhouse, 1589 (section relating to part of his library). (See p. 51.)

12. Charter of Edward I (1291/2) confirming the privileges of the university. Illuminated initial showing the King presenting the charter to (on the left, standing) a Doctor of Canon Law, wearing a 'cappa clausa' with two slits, and (on the right, standing) a Doctor of Civil Law, wearing the 'cappa manicata'. The two kneeling figures are Doctors of Theology (or Divinity) wearing the 'cappa clausa'. (See p. 54.)

13. From Robert Hare's transcripts, vol. I, fo. 276b, showing the survey of weights and measures. (See p. 57.)

14. Letters *temp*. Elizabeth I. Original order of Privy Council to Dr Preston, vice-chancellor, enforcing abstention from flesh in Lent, 18 March 1589/90. (See p. 65.)

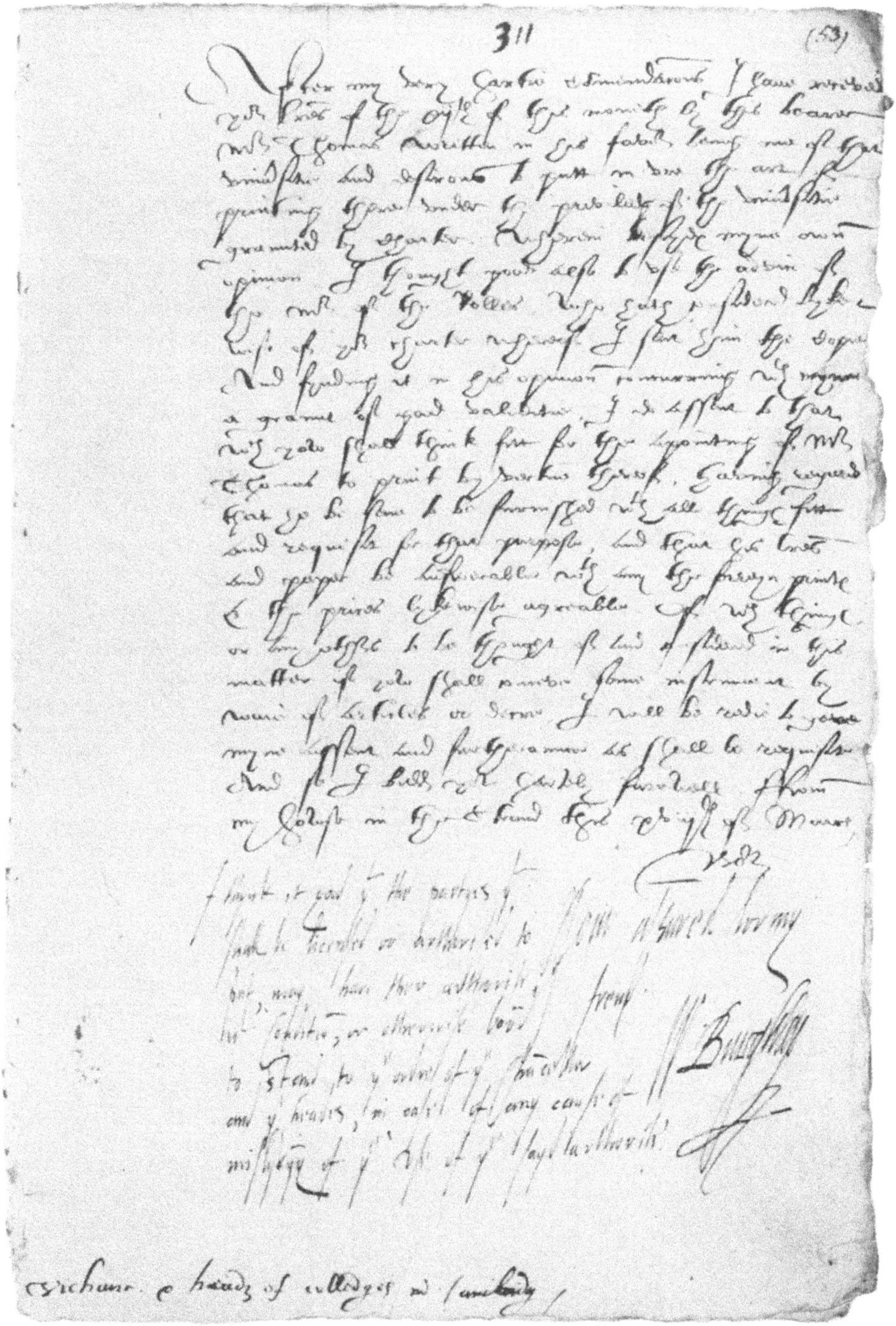

15. Letters *temp.* Elizabeth I. Burghley to vice-chancellor and heads concerning the establishment of a University Printing Office and appointing Mr Thomas as Printer, 18 March 1582/3. (See pp. 65 and 70n.)

Served In By The Order of E.q Camb hor of University
1705

April		£ s d
:14: Beef, Mutton, Veal, Suet And a Braune weight 169 Stone 11 pd		39:12:00
:: 10 prigs		03:03:00
:: 9 Oxes hoads		00:09:00
:: 8 Tongues 1 Udder		00:09:00
:: 4 Gang of Calfs Feet		00:01:00
:: 3 Gang of hogs Feet & Ears		00:01:06
:: Hog Beef		00:01:06
:: 3 Qurh Lambe		00:07:06
:: 2 Dozns of Chikings		00:10:00
:: 8 Dozns of Pigones		01:00:00
:: 4 pair of Team Pigones		00:04:06
:: 10 pound of Butter		00:09:00
:: 12 Marrow bones		00:06:00
:: 5 Calfs heads		00:10:00
:: 54 Calfs Sweet Breads		02:10:00
:: 12 Pallets		00:02:00
:: 24 Sheeps Tongues		00:04:00
:: 12 pair Lambe Stones		00:06:00
:: Cloth		00:01:04
:: 4 Quarh of Cream		00:02:00
:: Breast veal 8 pd		00:02:08
	The Summe	51:00:00

May. 10. 1705
Rec: then of Sr John Elly Vicechancellor
of the University of Cambridge the sum
of fifty one pounds in full of their
Bill for provision layd in to Trinity Collage
towards the entertainm't of their Ma ty
then I gave as above

£ s d
51.0.0

James ovendon

16. A receipted bill relating to the entertainment of Queen Anne
in Trinity College, 16 April 1705. (See p. 66.)

12. THE RELATIONS BETWEEN THE CROWN AND THE UNIVERSITY

Although the crown was the patron and protector of the university from the earliest times, as the series of royal charters shows, it was not until the sixteenth century that the crown and its chief ministers began to be very closely concerned with the details of policy and administration of the university. From the Act of Supremacy of 1534, the Tudor sovereigns, uniting the functions of temporal and ecclesiastical head, were able to use their prerogative and dispensing powers to exercise a greater degree of direct control over the activities of the university than had hitherto been the case. The Royal Injunctions of 1535 (of which no contemporary copy remains in the archives) and the Elizabethan statutes of 1570, compiled by Whitgift and laid down by the crown for the university,[1] are the most striking documents which bear witness to the new attitude. The former deals primarily with the content of university education and the latter, in addition to this, with the machinery of university administration. By the Act for the Incorporation of the Universities of 1571, the privileged, autonomous, corporate status of the universities both of Oxford and Cambridge was made dependent solely upon the crown (and the crown and parliament) instead of, as in former times, upon a heterogeneous collection of privileges, some of royal, some of ecclesiastical authority.

The concern of the sovereign that the ancient seats of learning should be centres of sound religion and morals, manners, and instruction is shown, particularly in the reigns of Elizabeth I and James I, by frequent personal letters, inquiries, and returns, directions and exhortations, sent to the vice-chancellor or to the university as a whole. The university archives have preserved original letters, some of them holograph, from the sovereign, the privy council, the secretaries of state, the ecclesiastical commissioners, and others, on a variety of subjects, from 1567 to 1601, as well as a series of letter-books, with copies of letters to and from the university, from 1506.[2] Religion is the matter which the central government had chiefly at heart, and a typical inquiry is that of 1591 concerning all persons from beyond sea, seminary priests, Jesuits, etc.,[3] to be circulated among the colleges and

[1] Plate 8.　　[2] 'Epistolae Academiae': 3 vols. Also Letters *temp.* Elizabeth I and James I (plates 14 and 15).
[3] C.U.R. 4 (Miscellanea), no. 1.

returned with answers to the vice-chancellor. (There is a similar inquiry, when anxiety about papists was again mounting in 1678.) The next most engrossing topic is the appearance and behaviour of the student population. This is regulated by a series of injunctions, from 'A Brief of Injunctions concerning Apparel from my Ld. Treasurer', 1588, through various detailed sets of instructions issued by James I and Charles I, on apparel, unsuitable sports and pastimes, bedmakers, and behaviour in chapel. The climax of these activities on the part of church and state would almost certainly have been the visitation of Archbishop Laud, had it taken place. The king in council decided in June 1636 in favour of Laud's right to visit as metropolitan, in spite of strenuous opposition from the university.[1] The university archives contain drafts and papers on the university's privileges, used in building up the case for exemption. Political and national controversies leave a remarkably small deposit in the archives, the crucial years 1640–3 bringing only a few copies of petitions, broad-sheets, and missives from either side.[2] Throughout the period there are letters concerned with appointments to offices, disputes with individuals, and the ever-recurrent friction with the town. But the personal letter, as a form of royal or governmental control and direct interference in university affairs, seems to decline equally with the use of the royal prerogative. It was not resumed to any great extent after the first few years immediately following the Restoration (except in so far as the sovereign continued to intervene in college elections), and its use became restricted to formal addresses and appointments.

From the succession of the Hanoverians, the exchange of letters directly between the university and the sovereign has been generally confined to loyal addresses, congratulations, and thanks for favours received.[3] The most recent addition to this class is the reply of Her Majesty, Queen Elizabeth II, to the loyal address of the university of Cambridge of 21 May 1952, signed with her own hand. There have also been the occasions of royal visits, from the famous visit of Elizabeth I in 1564 to those of our own day; and it is notable that the visits best documented in the archives have been those of sovereign queens, notably that of Queen Anne in 1705, and those of Queen Victoria in 1843 and 1847.[4]

[1] J. P. C. Roach, 'The University of Cambridge', *Victoria County History of Cambridgeshire*, vol. III, p. 198.
[2] C.U.R. 78 (University Miscellanea), nos. 60–64*b*.
[3] C.U.R. 24 (Addresses, 1715–1906).
[4] C.U.R. 27 (Royal, etc.—Visits, 1614–1904); also 'Visit of Queen Anne, 1705' (plate 16), and 'Visits of Queen Victoria 1843, 1847,' by registrary Romilly.

The withdrawal of the crown and its personal advisers from direct intervention in the affairs of the country and of the university did not mean that, in an era of parliamentary ascendancy, the university was completely free from the interference of the central government. On the contrary, it was subject to considerable indirect pressure, exercised through patronage and appointments to office, on the part of the men who manipulated the parliamentary machine. And in the smaller world of the university many of the facets of party and political controversy were reflected.

It may be said of Cambridge, during the middle years of the eighteenth century, that, though not prolific of great scholars, it was peculiarly rich in University politicians; and any society over which Newcastle [Chancellor of the University, 1748–1768] presided was not likely to lack opportunities of exercising its talents in the direction of intrigue and wire-pulling.[1]

Such activities, however, left little record in the official archives of the university.

When, in the middle of the nineteenth century, the winds of reform began to blow strongly through Cambridge, the powers of both crown and parliament were directly invoked, to assist and give authority to the radical revision of the constitution and practice of the university. The machinery used was that of royal and statutory commissions, orders in council, and acts of parliament. The reports of the royal commissions of 1850–2, which dealt with university affairs generally, and that of 1872–4, which dealt with university finance, the acts of parliament of 1856 and 1877, together with many supplementary papers, remain in the archives to record the complicated details of every stage of the process. After the First World War another royal commission was appointed (1919–22), followed by a statutory commission (1923–27); a few papers relating to these commissions have been preserved.

Today, the university's connection with the crown in council, in the matter of statute revision, has been maintained. New or revised statutes for the university (or indeed for any of the colleges) have to be approved by the queen in council. The privy council has a university committee to which proposed changes in university statutes are submitted. A formal notice of approval is sent by the secretary of the privy council to the registrary, and such notices are kept in the university registry for reference.

[1] D. A. Winstanley, *The University of Cambridge in the Eighteenth Century* (Cambridge, 1922), p. 1.

13. OTHER UNIVERSITY INSTITUTIONS AND THEIR RECORDS

The university has been the parent of several important institutions which, in course of time, have achieved a large measure of autonomy within the framework of university administration, and which now generally keep their own records. Their earlier records, however, cannot be properly differentiated from the main body of university archives, for they are to be found partly in the Grace Books, partly in the financial records of the university, and partly in the archives relating to the buildings which formerly housed them. The remainder, mainly in the form of loose papers, were bound up by registrary Luard in a series of guard-books. It should be noted that in some cases the first relevant documents in a guard-book are in fact earlier than the establishment of the institution concerned.

THE UNIVERSITY LIBRARY

In 1870 registrary Luard published *A Chronological List of Graces, Documents and Other Papers in the University Registry, which concern the University Library.* He drew on a variety of sources in the university archives, but principally upon the papers in the eight volumes of guard-books C.U.R. 31: 1–8 (Library). The contents of these volumes were, in February 1950, transferred to the university library, where they are being used by Mr J. C. T. Oates, an under-librarian, who is compiling a full-scale history of the university library.

THE UNIVERSITY PRESS

The largest collection of records relating to a university institution are those of the University Press. The greater part of these remained at the Press for some time after the rest of the university archives had moved to the Old Schools and, while there, were used for several notable publications on the history of Cambridge printing and publishing (see Appendix C, Select Bibliography). In 1957 all but the most modern records were deposited in the university archives, and these fall into two groups.

The first is the series of eight bound registry volumes numbered 33:1 to 33:8. These contain some 700 items ranging in date from the mid-sixteenth to the early twentieth century. They are arranged roughly as follows:

33:1.	University Printers	66 items	*c.* 1550–*c.* 1890;
33:2.	Privileges	120 items	*c.* 1590–*c.* 1730;
33:3.	Privileges	85 items	*c.* 1740–*c.* 1760;
33:4.	Privileges	63 items	*c.* 1780–*c.* 1880;
33:5.	Premises	45 items	*c.* 1720–*c.* 1890;
33:6.	Miscellaneous	87 items	*c.* 1550–*c.* 1750;
33:7.	Miscellaneous	125 items	*c.* 1740–*c.* 1890;
33:8.	Miscellaneous	114 items	*c.* 1890–*c.* 1930.

Each item is numbered and a manuscript list of contents is given at the front of each volume. A 'List of Papers and Documents Bound in Registry Volumes 33:1–33:8', compiled in 1951 by Mr G. A. Chinnery, is available in typescript, with index.

The second collection consists exclusively of the detailed business records of the Cambridge University Press from the late seventeenth to the early nineteenth century. It provides the earliest and the fullest documentation of any English printing-house of the hand-press period. There are three classes of document: the Minute Book of the Syndics of the Press for the period 1737–1824; a series of detailed annual income and expenditure accounts sheets; and a series of detailed printing-house vouchers. The Minute Book, which forms part of the volume Minutes of the Syndics, records the deliberations of the managing body. These were of two kinds: orders governing the management of the Press, and orders prescribing the prices charged to booksellers for the composition, printing, and correction of books produced for them. An earlier Minute Book, covering the years 1696–1714, 1725 and 1739–48, is held at the University Press. The annual income and expenditure accounts are statements of the amount and cost of work done during each vice-chancellor's year (November to November), of expenditure on supplies and maintenance, and of income received from booksellers. They run from 1698–9 to 1741–2, with gaps for the years 1700–1, 1705–6, 1706–7, and 1712–13 to 1716–17. The vouchers are, generally speaking, of two kinds. On the one hand are the bills submitted by the tradesmen or merchants who provided goods and services for the printing-house—joiners, plumbers, fellmongers and smiths, as well as paper merchants, inkmakers, and typefounders. This class of voucher begins in 1696 and continues for the whole of the eighteenth century. On the other hand, there are the receipts or receipted bills of the printing-house employees —compositors, pressmen, and correctors. This second class of voucher has survived only for the period from 1698 to 1744. A study of the Press, incorporating a transcription, with index, of all annual accounts sheets and all vouchers for the period 1696–1712, is in course of preparation by Dr D. F. McKenzie.

The series of annual accounts prepared by the vice-chancellor, the University Audit Books, the Grace Books, and the Acta of the vice-chancellor's court, also contain information about printing at Cambridge. Among miscellaneous papers not in either of the two main collections are the articles of agreement between the university and Thomas Thomas (1586),[1] a number of Press petitions (1614–24), a mid-seventeenth century book of imprimaturs, votes for university printers (1683–1802 and 1836), and the accounts of the financial management of Richard Watts (1802–8).

THE BOTANIC GARDENS

There are two volumes of papers, C.U.R. 25 (Botanic Gardens), relating to the Old Botanic Garden, running from 1717 to 1850, supplemented by two volumes of Botanic Gardens Accounts 1776–1854. The minutes and accounts of the New Botanic Gardens Syndicate, which supervised the transfer of the Gardens to their present site, are kept from 1854 to 1856. Substantial extracts from these volumes have been made by the director, Mr J. S. L. Gilmour, with a view to future publication.

THE OBSERVATORY

There is one volume of papers relating to the Observatory, C.U.R. 29 (Observatory), running from 1818 to 1878, supplemented by a Minute Book of the Observatory Syndicate, 1817–47.

THE FITZWILLIAM MUSEUM

The three guard-books of papers, C.U.R. 30: 1–3 (Fitzwilliam Museum), run from 1816 to 1911, and the Minute Book and Accounts of the Fitzwilliam Museum Syndicate from 1834 to 1853; accounts only from 1854 to 1883. There are also

[1] Letters *temp.* Elizabeth I contain a letter from Lord Burghley about Thomas's appointment (plate 15).

some documents relating to bequests, 1857–1912, and an amusing 'Memorial to the V.C. respecting pictures in the Fitzwilliam Museum, said to be of an immoral character, 1851'.

With regard to the building, there is a copy of the sketch for the abortive plan of 1824 to place the Museum on the site of Waterhouse's building, Caius College, and Basevi's plans submitted for competition and contract for the existing building, 1835–7.

OTHER UNIVERSITY BUILDINGS

Papers relating to the buildings on the Old Schools site were mainly bound into the guard-books C.U.R. 31 (Library) and details of Cockerell's building are found in the minutes and accounts of the New Library Syndicate, 1836–43. There are two volumes of papers relating to Great St Mary's Church (C.U.R. 18:1–2), covering the period 1575–1871. A volume on the Senate House (C.U.R. 46) covers various preliminary projects from 1673 and continues to 1889.

Museums and lecture rooms are dealt with in two volumes of papers (C.U.R. 55:1–2). These volumes include material relating both to the New Museums and to the earlier laboratories, built to house the expanding scientific studies of the university during the nineteenth century, and cover the dates from 1828 to 1889.

Material (other than minute books) relating to these departments whose head-quarters lie outside the buildings and sites already mentioned is not kept in the university archives. There are a number of minute books of syndicates, committees and boards dating from about 1737 to 1947 in the archives, and these have been listed in detail. Many of the more modern minute books are now kept by the secretaries of the university departments concerned, as are those of the various faculty boards.

APPENDICES

A. MAIN CLASSES OF MANUSCRIPT SOURCES IN THE ARCHIVES

THE UNIVERSITY AND COLLEGES AS PRIVILEGED CORPORATIONS (CH. IV)

(*a*) Charters of Privilege
From 50 Henry III.

(*b*) Statutes
1390 Earliest collection (copy probably replacing those destroyed in 1381).
1570 Great Elizabethan Code of Statutes.
1882 New Statutes.[1]

RECORDS OF UNIVERSITY ADMINISTRATION (CH. V)

(*a*) Grace Books
A–Y 1454–1880 (Graces printed in *University Reporter* after 1870).
Volumes A, B, Γ, Δ, are published, and cover the period 1454–1589.

(*b*) Orders of Vice-Chancellor and Heads (Notebooks of)
From 1750.

(*c*) Minutes of the Council of the Senate
From 1856.

RECORDS OF MATRICULATION AND DEGREES (CH. VI)

(*a*) Matriculations
1544 (gap 1590–1601) to present day.

(*b*) Ordo Senioritatis 1498/9 to 1746/7 and Triposes from 1747/8 to present day.
Published in *The Historical Register of the University of Cambridge*, and Supplements.

(*c*) The Supplicats
Certificates signed by college praelectors testifying to qualifications, residence, etc., of candidates for degrees, 1568–1870.

[1] The main body of the Statutes in force in 1962 was made by the University of Cambridge Commissioners in 1926 and 1927 and approved by His Majesty in Council in 1926–28.

(*d*) Subscription Books

Candidates for degrees were required to sign their acceptance of the royal supremacy and of the formularies of the Anglican Church.

1613–1833 (interrupted between 1642–60).

1833–70 (subscriptions to modified formula).

FINANCIAL RECORDS OF THE UNIVERSITY (CH. VII)
Detailed accounts from 1454: earliest in Grace Books

(*a*) Audit Books

1545–1880 (gap 1822–8).

(*b*) University Accounts

Vouchers (bound volumes), 1558–1700.

(*c*) Vice-Chancellor's Accounts and Vouchers

1575–1859 (unbound).

ENDOWMENTS OF THE UNIVERSITY (CH. VIII)
See Appendix B

RECORDS OF THE UNIVERSITY COURTS (CH. X)
The Vice-Chancellor's Court

(*a*) Act Books, 1552–1861.

(*b*) Books: Depositions, etc., 1591–1675.

(*c*) Files: 'Exhibita', 1559–1697.

The Vice-Chancellor's Probate Jurisdiction

(*a*) University wills (proved in the vice-chancellor's court), 1528–1765 and volumes of registered copies, 1501–1765.

(*b*) University Inventories, 1498–1761.

(*c*) University Administration Bonds, 1534–1746.

Commissary's Court

(*a*) Act Books, 1580–1746.

(*b*) Books: Depositions, 1580–1640.

(*c*) Files: 'Exhibita', 1580–1692.

(*d*) Acta at Sturbridge Fair, 1562–1855.

RECORDS OF UNIVERSITY JURISDICTION IN THE
TOWN OF CAMBRIDGE (CH. XI)

The Vice-Chancellor's Powers of Issuing Licences

(a) Ale-House Licences, 1616–1836.

(b) Licensing of Victuallers, 1596–1856.

(c) Lodging-House Licences, 1841–73.

Proctorial Jurisdiction

(a) Leet Rolls and Books, 1382–1782.

(b) Assize of Bread and Ale, etc., 1596–1836.

(c) Spinning-House Committals, 1823–94.

RELATIONS BETWEEN THE CROWN AND THE UNIVERSITY (CH. XII)

Royal Letters and Mandates

Elizabeth I to Victoria.

'GUARD-BOOKS' AND UNIVERSITY PAPERS

In addition to the classes of records mentioned above under chapter headings, there is the important series of 'guard-books'. These are an artificial class, arranged under 137 subject headings, and dating from the sixteenth to the twentieth century, formed by binding up loose papers from the registrary's office. Many of the volumes relate to university officers (see chapter 9), endowments, buildings, and the work of faculties and departments. It should also be mentioned that some documents relating to the colleges are to be found among the archives, particularly in the 'guard-books'.

There is also a series of bound volumes, entitled 'University Papers', beginning in 1774. These contain newspaper cuttings and other printed papers relating to university affairs.

B. MUNIMENTS OF TITLE RELATING TO UNIVERSITY PROPERTY

(N.B. It should be noted here that there is as yet no card-index of persons relating to these deeds and papers. There is, however, an index of places and lists of the parcels of property concerned, together with the names of the parties to the individual transactions, in some of the boxes.)

BEDFORDSHIRE

Thurleigh (Lucasian Professorship of Mathematics founded by Henry Lucas, 1663).
Deeds, 1666–1736.
Papers, 1642–1871.

CAMBRIDGESHIRE

Balsham (Plumian Professorship of Astronomy founded by the Rev. Thomas Plume, 1704).
Deeds, 1561–1876.
Papers, 1721–1884.

Barton (purchased by the university from Devereux Martin, Esq., of Barton, 1681).
Deeds, 1543–1933.
Papers, 1543–1894.

Burwell (rectory of Burwell St Mary purchased by the university from Lord North, 1544, and grant confirmed by royal letters patent 1544. Rectory of Burwell St Andrew purchased, 1646).
Deeds, 1381–1869.
Papers, 1540–1903.

Cottenham, Rampton and Over (benefaction of Thomas Hobson, 1628. For further details see J. W. Clark, *Endowments of the University of Cambridge*, pp. 558–65).
Map and a few nineteenth-century papers only.

Landbeach (benefaction of William Worts, 1709. For further details see J. W. Clark, *Endowments of the University of Cambridge*, pp. 89–93).
Deeds, 1744–1851.
Papers, 1709–1878.

CHESHIRE

Clive, Elworth, Sandbach and Middlewich (bequest of the estates of the Rev. John Hulse, 1790, to form the Hulse Trust, chiefly to further the teaching in divinity).
Deeds, 1328–1935.
Papers, 1647–1923.

Overton and Smallwood (Lowndean Professorship of Astronomy and Geometry, founded by Thomas Lowndes, 1748).
Deeds, 1582–1922.
Papers, 1664–1859.

APPENDICES

ESSEX

Ridgewell (or Riddiswell) (leased from St Catharine's College from 1680, to supplement income of Rustat Benefaction. See also Norfolk: Ovington).
Deeds, 1680–1780.
Papers, 1687–1754.

Writtle and Chelmsford (Knightbridge Professorship of Moral Theology or Casuistical Divinity, founded by the Rev. John Knightbridge, 1677. See also Hertfordshire: Therfield and Ashwell).
Papers, 1838–45.

HAMPSHIRE

Bishopstoke, Kilmeston and Neatham (in Binstead) (bequest by Lady Sadleir, 1706, for the endowment of Algebra lectures in the colleges. Conveyed to the university for the establishment of the Sadleirian Professorship of Mathematics, 1866. See also London: Eastcheap).
Deeds relating to Bishopstoke Farm (or Pile Hill), 1674–1866.
Papers relating to Bishopstoke Farm (or Pile Hill), 1674–1856.
Deeds relating to Kilmeston, 1640–1872.
Papers relating to Kilmeston, 1636–1918.
Terrier relating to Kilmeston, 1748.
Deeds relating to Neatham (in Binstead), 1590–1866.
Papers relating to Neatham (in Binstead), 1590–1854.

HERTFORDSHIRE

Therfield and Ashwell (Knightbridge Professorship of Moral Theology, founded by the Rev. John Knightbridge, 1677. Endowment increased by the Rev. Thomas Smoult, D.D., 1703. See also Essex: Writtle and Chelmsford).
Deeds relating to Therfield, 1838–74.
Papers relating to Therfield, 1838–74.
Papers relating to Ashwell, 1834–1947.

HUNTINGDONSHIRE

Somersham and Pidley (rectory of Somersham assigned to Regius Professorship of Divinity (founded 1540) by charter of James I, 1605. Disannexed by Act of Parliament, 1882, and income divided between Incumbent and Professor).
Deeds, 1784–1924.
Papers, 1724–1933.

LINCOLNSHIRE

Spalding, Manor of Fleet (estate purchased with part of benefaction of John Crane, 1651. For further details see J. W. Clark, *Endowments of the University*, pp. 565–70).
Deeds, 1656–1807.
Papers, 1618–1907.

LONDON

Eastcheap (house in) (part of bequest by Lady Sadleir, 1706. See also Hampshire: Bishopstoke, Kilmeston and Neatham (in Binstead)).
Deeds, 1611–1816.
Papers, 1631–1834.
Copies of deeds, 1539–1610.

NORFOLK

Ovington (Ovington manor and farm purchased with benefaction of £1000 made to the library by Tobias Rustat, 1667. See also Essex: Ridgewell (or Riddiswell)).
Court Rolls, *c.* 1330–*c.* 1645.
Rental Rolls, *c.* 1565–*c.* 1652.
Deeds, 1382–1938.
Papers, 1586–1949.

Raveningham and Thurlton (Woodwardian Professorship of Geology, founded by John Woodward, M.D., 1728).
Deeds, 1606–1940.
Papers, 1731–1939.

Terrington (rectorial tithes assigned to Lady Margaret Reader by charter of James I, 1605. Confirmed by Act of Parliament, 1712. In 1860, greater part of Terrington tithes assigned to Norrisian Professor of Divinity by statute, and confirmed by the Queen in Council).
Terrier, eighteenth century.
Papers, 1649–1877.

NORTHAMPTONSHIRE

Kislingbury (rents of estate bequeathed by the Rev. Thomas Seaton, 1748, to found a prize to be awarded to an M.A. for the best poem on a sacred subject).
Deeds, 1627–1876.
Papers, 1699–1863.

SOMERSET

Bishop Sutton in Chew Magna (part of estate left by John Stewart of Rannoch, 1884, to found scholarships. For further details see J. W. Clark, *Endowments of the University*, pp. 335–7).

77

Deeds, 1729–1845.
Papers, 1881–1919.

Keynsham (part of estate left by John Stewart of Rannoch to found scholarships).
Deeds, 1771–1825.
Papers, 1881–1885.

SUFFOLK

Brettenham and Hitcham (parcels of land given to endow scholarships by William
Battie, M.D., 1747).
Papers, 1747–1948.

SUSSEX

East Grinstead and Hartfield, Manor of Cansern (bequest of John Lord Craven, 1649,
to found four scholarships, two at Oxford, and two at Cambridge. For further
details see J. W. Clark, *Endowments of the University*, pp. 286–94).
Copy of will dated 1647.
Copy of indenture dated 1664.
Estate map, 1724.

C. SELECT BIBLIOGRAPHY, 1785-1961

(C. = Calendar; E. = Extracts; O. = Original Language; T. = Translation)

I. PUBLICATIONS OF DOCUMENTS RELATING TO THE UNIVERSITY
OF CAMBRIDGE COMPILED FROM THE CENTRAL RECORDS, TRAN-
SCRIPTS OR PRINTED SOURCES (1785–1912)

[The following are the sources most frequently used:

(1) MSS. Hare, in the university archives. These transcripts, presented to the university
in 1587 by Robert Hare, were compiled from both the central records and the
university charters.
(2) MSS. Baker vols. 1–23 in the British Museum, and vols. 24–42 and A–D in the
university library.
(3) The Parker Collection in Corpus Christi College, Cambridge.
(4) The printed *Statuta* of 1785 (see below).
(5) Acts of Parliament.]

George Dyer, *History of the University and Colleges of Cambridge* ... (2 vols., London 1814). Based on transcripts by F. S. Parris and others.

George Dyer, *The Privileges of the University of Cambridge; together with Additional Observations on its History, Antiquities, Literature, and Biography* (2 vols., London, 1824). Transcripts from MSS. Hare, Statuta, etc. O.E.T.

John Lamb (ed.), *A Collection of Letters, Statutes, and other Documents from the Manuscript Library of Corpus Christi College, illustrative of the History of the University of Cambridge...from A.D. MD, to A.D. MDLXXII* (London, 1838). From transcripts of the Parker Collection. O.E.

James Heywood (ed.), *Collection of Statutes for the University and the Colleges of Cambridge...* (London, 1840). T.

George Peacock, *Observations on the Statutes of the University of Cambridge* (London and Cambridge, 1841). From the Statuta, MSS. Hare, and MSS. Cole. O.E.

Charles Henry Cooper, *Annals of Cambridge* (5 vols., Cambridge, 1842–1908). From the Statuta, MSS. Hare and other transcripts. E.T.

Documents relating to the University and Colleges of Cambridge, published by direction of the Commissioners appointed by the Queen...(3 vols., London, 1852). Vol. 1 contains: Abstract of Records in the Central Repositories relating to the University of Cambridge and Statuta Antiqua and Elizabethan Statutes of 1570 (from the Statuta, collated with the Proctors' Books in the university archives). O.E.C.

James Heywood and Thomas Wright (eds.), *Cambridge University Transactions during the Puritan Controversies of the 16th and 17th Centuries* (2 vols., London, 1854). From MSS. Lansdowne in the British Museum and other transcripts. O.E.

James Heywood (ed.), *Early Cambridge University and College Statutes in the English Language* (London, 1855). T.

John Griffiths (ed.), *Enactments in Parliament specially concerning the Universities of Oxford and Cambridge* (Oxford, 1869). O.E.

John Willis Clark (ed.), *Letters Patent of Elizabeth and James the First addressed to the University of Cambridge, with other Documents* (with a translation of the letters of Elizabeth and an appendix of earlier grants referred to therein) (Cambridge, 1892). O.T.

William Baillie Skene (ed.), *Handbook of certain Acts affecting the Universities of Oxford and Cambridge and the Colleges therein in the Sale, Acquisition and Administration of Property* (London, 1894). O.E.

Lionel Lancelot Shadwell (ed.), *Enactments in Parliament specially concerning the Universities of Oxford and Cambridge...1363–1910*, Oxford Historical Society, vols. 58–61 (Oxford, 1911–12). O.E.

II. PUBLICATIONS OF THE UNIVERSITY, CALENDARS, LISTS AND NOTICES BASED UPON MATERIAL IN THE UNIVERSITY ARCHIVES (1684–1961)

Statuta quædam Academiae Cantabrigiensis in admissione ad Gradus, &c...Cantabrigiae 1684. [John Hayes, University Printer] [followed by tables of fees for the various degrees and the cycle of proctors 1660–1716].

Statuta Academiæ Cantabrigiensis (Cambridge, 1785). The first printed edition of the statutes, limited to thirty-five copies. There have been various subsequent editions of the statutes based on this text.

Statuta Academiae Cantabrigiensis (Cambridge, 1859). The first editions, 1849–58, were printed for the use of the Revision Syndicate only. The editions appearing in 1859 and 1861 were prefaced by the act of 1856, and an act of 1858 repealing stamp duties on matriculations and degrees. Various paper-bound editions appeared between 1859 and 1882.

Ordinationes Academiæ Cantabrigiensis (Cambridge, 1859). The first collection, 1858, compiled by Dr Henry Philpott, was printed for the use of the council of the senate. Subsequent editions of the ordinances were published periodically until 1939, with supplements annually.

Statutes of the University of Cambridge with some Acts of Parliament relating to the University (Cambridge, 1882). New ed. 1896.

Statutes for the University of Cambridge and for the Colleges within it...(Cambridge, 1883).

Statutes of the University of Cambridge...and *Ordinances of the University of Cambridge to 1 October 1904* (2 vols., Cambridge, 1904), ed. John Willis Clark. Supplements issued triennially to 1914.

Statutes for the University of Cambridge made by the University of Cambridge Commissioners (Cambridge, 1926). Re-issued periodically until 1946.

Statutes and Ordinances were issued together from 1946.

Lists of *Graduati* have been compiled from the registers by registrary Borlase in 1787 and 1800, registrary Hustler in 1823, registrary Romilly in 1846 and 1856, registrary Luard in 1873 and 1884. These are arranged chronologically.

The Book of Matriculations and Degrees: A Catalogue of those who have been Matriculated or been admitted to any Degree in the University of Cambridge from 1544 to 1659, ed. John Venn and J. A. Venn (Cambridge, 1913). Arranged alphabetically.

The Book of Matriculations and Degrees: A Catalogue of those who have been Matriculated or admitted to any Degree in the University of Cambridge from 1851 to 1900 [ed. John Willis Clark, Registrary and J. F. E. Faning] (Cambridge, 1902). Arranged alphabetically.

The Book of Matriculations and Degrees: A Catalogue of those who have been Matriculated or admitted to any Degree in the University of Cambridge from 1901 to 1912 [ed. John Neville Keynes, Registrary, B. Benham, and C. J. Stonebridge] (Cambridge, 1915). Arranged alphabetically.

Alumni Cantabrigienses...compiled by John Venn and J. A. Venn. Part I: Earliest times to 1751 (4 vols., Cambridge, 1922–7). Part II: 1752–1900 (6 vols., Cambridge, 1940–54). Arranged alphabetically and incorporating material from many other biographical sources.

The Cambridge University Calendar, first issued 1796–7, ed. G. Mackenzie. Published annually from 1799 to 1914, when the proprietorship was transferred to the University Press Syndics: see note in Introduction to *The Historical Register*.

The Cambridge University Register and Almanack for 1843, ed. W. A. Warwick. 'To be published annually' (Cambridge). Enlarged edition 1844.

The Cambridge University General Almanack and Register. Published annually 1856–77, by H. Wallis, Sidney Street, Cambridge.

The Cambridge University Calendar. Issued by the Syndics of the Press from 1914. Became *The Annual Register* in 1951–2.

The Historical Register of the University of Cambridge being a supplement to the Calendar with a record of university offices, honours and distinctions to the year 1910, ed. J. R. Tanner (Cambridge, 1917). Includes Ordo Senioritatis (from 1498/9 to 1746/7), Tripos Lists (from 1747/8 to 1910).

Index to Tripos Lists (1748–1910)..., compiled by C. W. Previté-Orton (Cambridge, 1923).

Supplements to The Historical Register, issued for 1911–20, 1921–30, 1931–40, 1941–50, 1951–5.

Trusts, Statutes and Directions affecting the Professorships, Scholarships and Prizes and Other Endowments of the University of Cambridge (Cambridge, 1857). Enlarged edition. 1876.

Endowments of the University of Cambridge, ed. John Willis Clark (Cambridge, 1904). Incorporating more documents and explanatory notes.

Calendar of Wills proved in Vice-Chancellor's Court at Cambridge, 1501–1765. [H. Roberts.] (Cambridge, 1907). Arranged alphabetically.

Cambridge University Polls, 1780–1869. Polls for the election of the two university representatives. Although printed separately after each election, these are usually found bound in sets.

The Poll at the Election of a Chancellor, 1847, ed. H. Gunning.

A Chronological List of the Graces, Documents, and Other Papers in the University Registry which concern the University Library, ed. for the Press Syndics (Cambridge, 1870).

First Report of the Royal Commission on Historical Manuscripts, 1870. Pages 73–4 contain a description of some of the bound volumes in the university archives.

The Cambridge Chronicle and University Journal, Isle of Ely Herald and Huntingdonshire Gazette. From its first issue on 30 October 1762, it had included a good deal of university and college news. From January 1849 printed in term, in the section 'University Journal', university lists, reports, notices, etc., which towards the end of the century were supplemented and gradually replaced by unofficial reports from its own correspondent.

The Cambridge University Reporter. From 19 October 1870 to 18 December 1872, published every Wednesday in term by Messrs Rivington, 19 Trinity Street, Cambridge. From 14 January 1873, published by authority. The official journal of the university.

III. PUBLICATIONS OF THE CAMBRIDGE ANTIQUARIAN SOCIETY
(Using material now in the university archives)

(a) Communications or Proceedings

C. Hardwick, 'Articuli Universitatis Cantabrigiæ': a form of petition addressed to King Henry V...(from MSS. Hare), vol. I (O.S.), no. XIX (pp. 85–93).

C. H. Cooper, 'On the earlier High Stewards of the University of Cambridge', vol. I (O.S.), no. XXXIV (pp. 273–8).

T. Brocklebank, 'Sir Robert Rede', vol. I (O.S.), no. XLIII (pp. 366–74).

H. Bradshaw, 'Two Lists of Books in the University Library', vol. II (O.S.), no. XXII (from 'Registrum Librorum' with section on University Cross) (pp. 239–78).

H. R. Luard, 'A Letter from Bishop Bale to Archbishop Parker' (formerly C.U.R. 8, Misc. no. 2 *now* U.L.C. MS. Add. 7489), vol. III (O.S.), no. XI (pp. 157–73).

H. R. Luard, 'A Letter to the University from Thomas Beaufort, Duke of Exeter' (Document 95), vol. III (O.S.), no. XXV (pp. 273–4).

H. Bradshaw, 'On the Collection of Portraits belonging to the University before the Civil War', vol. III (O.S.), no. XXVI (pp. 275–86).

H. R. Luard, 'A List of the Documents in the University Registry, from the year 1266 to the year 1544', vol. III (O.S.), no. XXXVIII (pp. 385–403).

R. Bowes, 'Biographical Notes on the University Printers...', vol. V (O.S.), no. XX (pp. 283–362).

W. H. St John Hope, 'On the Armorial Ensigns of the University and Colleges of Cambridge, and of the Five Regius Professors', vol. VIII (O.S.), no. XXXV (pp. 107–33).

C. J. B. Gaskoin, 'The University Wills at Peterborough', vol. X (O.S.), no. XLIV (pp. 314–16).

J. W. Clark, 'On the Charitable Foundations in the University called Chests;...'
(with Document 35), vol. XI (O.S.), no. XLV (pp. 78–101).

H. P. Stokes, 'Early University Property' (with Document 16), vol. XIII (O.S.), no. LIII
(pp. 164–84).

W. M. Palmer, 'College Dons, Country Clergy, and University Coachmen', vol. XVI
(O.S.), no. LXIII (pp. 145–96).

A. S. F. Gow, 'A Cambridge Seal-box of the Seventeenth Century', vol. XXXIV
(pp. 59–76).

(b) Octavo Publications

H. P. Stokes, *The Chaplains and the Chapel of the University of Cambridge (1256–1568)*,
no. XLI (1906). With portions of 'Registrum Librorum', etc.

J. W. Clark, *The Riot at the Great Gate of Trinity College, February 1610–11*, no. XLIII
(1906). From 'Acta Curiae'.

H. P. Stokes, *The Esquire Bedells of the University of Cambridge*, no. XLV (1911).

H. P. Stokes, *The Mediæval Hostels of the University of Cambridge*, no. XLIX (1924).

IV. PUBLICATIONS INCORPORATING MATERIAL FROM DOCUMENTS IN THE UNIVERSITY ARCHIVES, 1785–1949

John Beverley, *An Account of the Different Ceremonies observed in the Senate House of the University of Cambridge*...(Cambridge, 1788). E. This prints, e.g. decrees; see
pp. 161–2.

Adam Wall, *An Account of the Different Ceremonies observed in the Senate House of the University of Cambridge*;...(Cambridge, 1798). E.

Henry Gunning (ed.), *The Ceremonies observed in the Senate House of the University of Cambridge*.... A new edition of the above (Cambridge, 1828). E.

William Frend, *An Account of the Proceedings in the University of Cambridge, against William Frend, M.A., Fellow of Jesus College, Cambridge, for publishing a pamphlet, entitled Peace and Union, etc.*...(Cambridge, 1793). E.

A Sequel to the Account of the Proceedings...(etc.) (London, 1795). E.

[Gilbert Ainslie], *An Historical Account of the Oaths and Subscriptions required in the University of Cambridge on Matriculation, and of all persons who proceed to the degree of Master of Arts* (Cambridge, 1833). O.E.

Henry Gunning, *Reminiscences of the University, Town, and County of Cambridge, from the year 1780* (2 vols., London, 1854). E. Contains material supplied by registrary
Romilly from the archives.

James Bass Mullinger, *The University of Cambridge* (3 vols., Cambridge, 1873–1911).
O.E. Appendix A to vol. III contains 'Electio Cancellarii 1 Jun. 1626'.

Christopher Wordsworth, *Social Life at the English Universities in the Eighteenth Century* (Cambridge, 1874). E.

Christopher Wordsworth, *Scholae Academicae: Some Account of the Studies at the English Universities in the Eighteenth Century* (Cambridge, 1877). E.

Robert Willis and John Willis Clark, *The Architectural History of the University of Cambridge, and of the Colleges of Cambridge and Eton* (4 vols., Cambridge, 1886). Vol. III refers to documents nos. 77, 100, 128, 129. O.E.T.

Grace Book A, ed. S. M. Leathes (1897). (Luard Memorial Series.) O.

Grace Book B (Part I and Part II), ed. M. Bateson (1903 and 1905). (Luard Memorial Series.) O.

Grace Book Γ, ed. W. G. Searle (1908). O.

Grace Book Δ, ed. John Venn (1910). O.

George J. Gray, *The Earlier Cambridge Stationers and Bookbinders and The First Cambridge Printer* (Oxford: The Bibliographical Society, 1904). O.

George J. Gray and William Mortlock Palmer, *Abstracts from the Wills and Testamentary Documents of Printers, Binders, and Stationers of Cambridge, from 1504 to 1699* (London: The Bibliographical Society, 1915). O.

Charles Sayle, *Annals of Cambridge University Library 1278–1900* (reprinted from *The Library* of 1915). (Cambridge, 1916.) E. Contains Proctors' Accounts, etc.

W. W. Rouse Ball, 'The Mathematical Tripos'. *Cambridge Papers*, pp. 252–316 (London, 1918).

S. C. Roberts, *A History of the Cambridge University Press, 1521–1921* (Cambridge, 1921). O.E.

H. P. Stokes, *Ceremonies of the University of Cambridge* (Cambridge, 1927).

D. A. Winstanley, *Unreformed Cambridge* (Cambridge, 1935). E.

W. D. Bushell, *Hobson's Conduit: The New River at Cambridge commonly called Hobson's River* (Cambridge, 1938). O.E. Appendix IV contains copy of part of 'An Order of a Court of Sewers', 1634.

E. A. Crutchley, *A History and Description of the Pitt Press*...(Cambridge, 1938).

D. A. Winstanley, *Early Victorian Cambridge* (Cambridge, 1940). O.E.

D. A. Winstanley, *Later Victorian Cambridge* (Cambridge, 1947). O.E.

W. D. Bushell, *The Church of St Mary the Great, the University Church at Cambridge* (Cambridge, 1948). E.

V. PUBLICATIONS INCORPORATING MATERIAL FROM THE UNIVERSITY ARCHIVES AND PUBLISHED SINCE THE ESTABLISHMENT OF THE KEEPERSHIP OF THE ARCHIVES, 1951–62

(a) Books

John R. H. Moorman, *The Grey Friars in Cambridge 1225–1538* (the Birkbeck Lectures for 1948–9, Cambridge, 1952). Discusses the controversy leading to the concord of 1306. (Document no. 13.)

E. F. Jacob, 'English University Clerks in the Later Middle Ages': 2. 'Petitions for Benefices from English Universities during the Great Schism' (pp. 223–39). Reprinted in *Essays in the Conciliar Epoch* (new edition: Manchester, 1953). The latter describes, from the papers of the late Dr A. H. Lloyd, the rolls forming document no. 82a.

J. W. Goodison, *Catalogue of Cambridge Portraits* I, The University Collection (Cambridge, 1955).

S. C. Roberts, *The Evolution of Cambridge Publishing* (the Sandars Lectures for 1954, Cambridge, 1956). Based on the Press archives and including plates illustrating some of them.

H. C. Porter, *Reformation and Reaction in Tudor Cambridge* (Cambridge, 1958). Contains a detailed note on the manuscripts in the university archives which are used in this work and an excellent Cambridge bibliography.

The City and University of Cambridge (*The Victoria History of the County of Cambridge and the Isle of Ely*, vol. III, London, 1959).

 Particularly the following articles:

 Helen M. Cam, 'The City of Cambridge' (pp. 1–149).

 J. P. C. Roach, 'The University of Cambridge' (pp. 150–312).

 J. P. C. Roach, 'The Schools and the University Library' (pp. 312–21).

 S. C. Roberts, 'The University Press' (pp. 321–4).

 C. R. Elrington, 'The Archives of the University of Cambridge' (pp. 327–9).

 C. R. Elrington, 'Seals and Insignia of Cambridge University and its Officers' (pp. 330–1).

Mark H. Curtis, *Oxford and Cambridge in Transition, 1558–1642: An Essay on changing Relations between the English Universities and English Society* (Oxford, 1959).

A. N. L. Munby, *Cambridge College Libraries: Aids for Research Students* (Cambridge, 2nd ed. 1962), pp. 52–5.

A. B. Emden, *A Biographical Register of the University of Cambridge to 1500* (in the press).

(b) Periodicals

C. P. Murrell (Mrs C. P. Hall), 'The Plague in Cambridge 1665–6', *The Cambridge Review*, vol. LXXII, nos. 1759–60 (1951).

J. C. T. Oates, 'Cambridge Books of Congratulatory Verses, 1603–1640, and their Binders', *Transactions of the Cambridge Bibliographical Society*, vol. I, part 5 (1953).

Hugh Tait, 'The Hearse-cloth of Henry VII belonging to the University of Cambridge', *Journal of the Warburg and Courtauld Institutes*, vol. XIX, nos. 3–4 (1956).

Cyprian Blagden, 'Early Cambridge Printers and the Stationers' Company', *Transactions of the Cambridge Bibliographical Society*, vol. II, 4 (1957).

J. C. T. Oates, 'The Deposit of Books at Cambridge under the Licensing Acts 1662–79, 1685–95', *Transactions of the Cambridge Bibliographical Society*, vol. II, 4 (1957).

R. Williamson, 'The Plague in Cambridge', *Medical History*, vol. I, no. 1 (1957).

H. E. Peek, 'An Introduction to the Archives of the University of Cambridge', *The Genealogists' Magazine*, vol. XII, no. 14 (June 1958) and vol. XII, no. 15 (September 1958).

Walter Ullmann, 'The University and the Great Schism', *Journal of Theological Studies*, vol. IX, part 1 (1958).

Walter Ullmann, 'The Decline of the Chancellor's Authority in Medieval Cambridge: A Rediscovered Statute', *The Historical Journal*, vol. I, no. 2 (1958).

D. F. McKenzie, 'Press-Figures: A Case History of 1701–1703' and 'Notes on Printing at Cambridge c. 1590', *Transactions of the Cambridge Bibliographical Society*, vol. III, part 1 (1959).

John Carter, 'William Ged and the Invention of Stereotype', *The Library*, 5th ser. vol. XV, no. 3 (1960).

A. Fairbank and B. Dickins, 'The Italic Hand in Tudor Cambridge', *Cambridge Bibliographical Society*, Monograph, no 5 (in the press).

INDEX

Accounts, 34-6, 73; Audit Books of, 10, 10 n., 19 n., 34, 35, 70, 73; Botanic Gardens, 70; Fitzwilliam Museum, 70; New Library Syndicate, 71; Press, 35, 69-70; Vouchers to, 36, 47, 69-70

'Acta Curiae' (Act Books), 8, 11, 12, 50, 70, 73

Act, of Supremacy (1534), 65; Paving— (1544), 62; — for the Incorporation of the Universities (1571), 15, 49, 65; Cam Navigation — (1851), 64; Cambridge Improvement — (1851), 61; Cambridge University and Town Waterworks — (1853), 63; Cambridge Award — (1856), 52, 53, 55, 60, 64; Universities Tests — (1871), 32; Cambridge Corporation — (1889), 64; Cambridge University and Corporation — (1894), 61; Universities and College Estates — (1925), 36

Acts of Parliament, 27, 67

Adams, Sir Thomas, 41

Addenbrooke's Hospital, 64

Ainslie, Dr Gilbert, master of Pembroke College [vice-chancellor], 32, 32 n.

Anne, Queen, 66, 66 n.

Arbitration, of the Lord Edward (1270), 25, 54, 54 n.

Ashton, Dr Charles [master of Jesus College], vice-chancellor, 43

Assize of Bread, etc., 12, 54, 55-7, 74

Award, of the Lady Margaret (1502/3), 58, 59; of Sir John Patteson (1855), 43, 55

Aylmer, John, 5

Basevi, George, 71

Battie, Dr William, benefactor, 78

Beale, Dr Jerome, master of Pembroke College and vice-chancellor, 16

Beaufort, Thomas, Duke of Exeter, 32

Bedell, 28, 58; Esquire Bedell, 7, 8, 10, 19 n., 28, 44-7 passim, 45 n.; Yeoman Bedell, 19 n., 48; see also Mere, John, and Stokys, Matthew

Benefactions, see Endowments

Benefactors, Commemoration of, 3, 18, 18 n., 26, 37-8, 38 n., 39

Botanic Gardens, 70

Browne, Bishop George Forrest, 29, 29 n.

Burwell, Rectory and Vicarage, 17, 39, 43, 75

Butts, Dr Henry [master of Corpus Christi College], vice-chancellor, 13, 62

Caius, Dr John [master of Gonville and Caius College], 31

Cambridge, town of, 2, 14, 25, 53-64 passim, 66, 74

Cambridge University Reporter, 22 n., 23, 29, 37, 72

Caput, 29, 30

Caryl, Dr Lynford, registrary [master of Jesus College and vice-chancellor], 20

Catalogue of the Archives, Caryl's, 20; Luard's, 25; Romilly's, 22; Rysley's, 4, 5, 5 n., 6, 17 n., 18, 39; Wren's, 17, 18, 39

Cecil, Sir Robert, chancellor, 33, 49

Cecil, William, Lord Burghley, chancellor, 33, 63

Chancellor, of the university, 5, 24, 30, 42, 44, 47, 49, 57, 59; Cecil, Sir Robert, 33, 49; Cecil, William, Lord Burghley, 33, 63; Colville, William, 25; Cromwell, Thomas, 34, 35; Fisher, Bishop John, 44; Pelham, Thomas, Duke of Newcastle, 67; Zouche, Eudo [? Guy] de la, 3

Chaplyn, Thomas, 63

Charities and Charitable Institutions: Addenbrooke's Hospital, 64; Crane's Charity, 40, 77; Hobson's Charity, 59, 61; Stokys' Alms Houses, 64; Storey's Charity, 64, Worts' Endowment, 64, 75; Wray's Charity, 64

Charles I, 26, 33, 66

Charles II, 32, 33

Charters of Privilege, 1-6 passim, 11, 15-19, 24-6, 43, 45, 47, 48, 53, 59, 65, 72

Chest, Common, of the university alias University Chest, 1-6 passim, 15, 16, 19, 35; Chest of Evidences, 6; Neel Chest, 2

Clark, John Willis, registrary, 22, 41

Close Rolls, 24, 24 n.

Colleges: Peterhouse, 17, 63; Clare, 16, 26, 41; Pembroke, 16, 17, 22, 26, 32; Gonville and Caius, 16; Trinity Hall, 11, 26; Corpus Christi, 3 n., 8, 8 n., 10, 39, 39 n., 40, 62; King's, 7, 8, 21-2, 39; St Catharine's, 29, 41; Jesus, 20, 38; St John's, 13; Trinity, 22, 40

Colleges, muniments of, 24, 39

Colleges, statutes of, 26, 27

Colville, Dr William, chancellor [master of Michaelhouse], 25

Commissary, 47, 49, 50, 52, 56, 73

Commission, of the university, to draw up roll of benefactors, 18; to review the muniments, 15-17

Commissioners, documents printed by royal, 1 n., 3 n., 27 n.; Ecclesiastical, 65; Improvement, 60, 64; of sewers, 63

Commissions, royal and statutory, 51, 67

Common Chest or University Chest, *see* Chest, Common

Commonwealth, 19

Cosin, Dr John [master of Peterhouse, vice-chancellor and bishop], 17

Council, *see* King in Council; Queen in Council

Council of the Senate, 23, 30, 32 n., 72

Court, Consistory, 10, 49

Courts of the university, 48-52, 73

Crane, John, benefactor, 40, 77

Craven, John Lord, benefactor, 78

Cromwell, Thomas [Earl of Essex and chancellor], 34, 35

Davers, Mrs Alice, benefactor, 40

Degrees, records of, 31-4, 72-3

Divinity Schools, 3

Edward, Arbitration of the Lord (1270), 25, 54, 54 n.

Edward I, 54, 54 n.

Edward VI, 18

Elizabeth I, 13, 26, 33, 48, 65, 65 n., 66; charters of, 11, 18, 26; statutes of, *see* statutes

Elizabeth II, 66

Elsden, Jane, 61

Endowments, 26, 37-41, *see* Appendix B, 74-8; dependence of provision for university teaching upon, 41; publication of deeds relating to, 41, 41 n.

Essex Cup, 43

Eugenius IV, 25

Fairs, jurisdiction at, 50, 55-6, 73; proclamation of, 55

Fisher, Dr John [master of Michaelhouse and president of Queens' College], senior proctor, 6, 7; vice-chancellor, 7; bishop and chancellor, 44

Fitzwilliam Museum, 38, 70-1

Gostlin, Dr John, master of Gonville and Caius College [vice-chancellor], 16

Grace Books, 7, 12, 23, 27, 28, 31, 34, 43, 68, 70, 72
A, 4, 6, 6 n., 8, 8 n., 23, 27, 28, 34, 47, 47 n., 54 n.
B, 6, 23, 27, 28, 34, 34 n.
Γ, 1 n., 7, 7 n., 8 n., 28
Δ, 8, 8 n., 15 n., 28, 31
E, 16 n.
Z, 16 n.

H, 13 n., 19 n.

Θ, 20 n.

N, 21 n., 22 n.

Gunning, Henry, [bedell], 47 n., 54, 56 n.

Hackett, Rev. Dr Benedict, 26-7

Hare, Robert, 15, 16, 44; transcripts of, 12, 12 n., 16, 18, 26, 44, 54, 57

Heedon, *alias* de Heydon, Roger, 5, 39

Henry III, 5

Henry V, 5

Henry VII, 25, 38

Henry VIII, 34, 38, 47

High Steward, 11, 49, 50

Hobbys, Robert, bedell, registrary, 7-8, 28

Hobson, Thomas, benefactor, 75

'Hobson's Brook', or 'New River', 63

Hobson's Charity Trust, 59, 61, *see also* Spinning House

Honorius I, 25

Hopkins, Daisy, 61

Hugo, bishop of Ely, 25

Hulse, the Rev. John, benefactor, 75

Hustler, William, registrary, 21

Jegon, Dr John [master of Corpus Christi College, vice-chancellor and bishop], 11, 58 n.

James I, 18, 26, 31, 56, 59, 65, 65 n., 66, 76, 77

James II, 33

Kelsal, Thomas, 39

Kemp v. Neville, 60

King in Council, 52

King's Ditch, 63

Knightbridge, the Rev. Dr John, benefactor, 76

Langbaine, Dr Gerard, 20

Laud, Archbishop William, proposed visitation of, 11, 18, 66

Leet, Black, 54, 56, 62; Paving, 56, 62, 64; Proctors', 50, 56, 62; records of, 11, 12, 56, 56 n., 74

Letters, latin, of the university, 46, 65, 65 n., 66; mandatory, from the sovereign and others, 32-3, 65, 74

Librarian, 45, 58

Library, 20, 40, 68; New Library Syndicate, 71

Licensing of victuallers, vintners, 56, 74

Lowndes, Thomas, benefactor, 75

Luard, Dr Henry Richards, registrary, 22, 23, 32 n., 68

Lucas, benefactor, Henry, 75

Manchester, Earl of, *see* Montagu, Henry

Mandates, for degrees, 32-3, 74

Margaret, Lady, 25, 38, 58; Lady Margaret's Professor, 8, 40; Lecturer and Preacher, 17; Reader, 38, 77

Marshal, University, 48

Mary I, 15

Matriculation, records of, 30-1, 72; registers of, 8, 11, 30, 58-9

Mayor, of Cambridge, 2, 2 n., 3 n., 34, 49, 55, 62

Measures, standard, of the university, 50, 55-7

Mere, John, bedell, benefactor, registrary, 8, 9, 12, 17, 38-40, 46-7, 54, 54 n.

Montagu, Henry, Earl of Manchester, high steward, 11

Mowse, Dr William [master of Trinity Hall], 16

Muniments of Title, *see* Supplementary Index

Museums, and lecture rooms, papers relating to, 71
    Ashmolean Museum, 38; Cambridge Museum of Archaeology and Ethnology, 57; Fitzwilliam Museum, 38, 70-1; Science Museum, South Kensington, 57

Neel Chest, 2

'New Chapel' of the university (or Regent House), 3, 15 n., 19, 20, 39 n., 45 n.

North, John, 31 n.

North, Lord, 75

Observatory, papers relating to, 70

'Old Schools', 3, 4, 10, 17, 19, 19 n., 21, 23, 39, 49; papers relating to site and buildings of, 71

Orator, public, of the university, 45, 46

'Orders of Vice-Chancellor and Heads', 30, 72

'Ordo Senioritatis', 7, 12, 31, 72

Oxford, university of, 2, 16, 24, 26, 29, 65; Ashmolean Museum, 38; church of St Mary the Virgin, 2; incorporation from, 34

[*Oxford*] *University Archives. A Lecture on the History of the*, vii, 2 n., 19 n., 20 n.

Oxford University Archives, keeper of the, vii, 20; registers of the, 6, 59; wills, book lists among the inventories of, 51

Palmerston, Viscount, *see* Temple, Henry John

Parker, Dr Matthew, Archbishop and benefactor [formerly master of Corpus Christi College and vice-chancellor], 3, 17, 40

Paske, Dr Thomas, master of Clare College [vice-chancellor], 16

Patteson, Sir John, Award of (1855), 43, 55

Pelham, Thomas, Duke of Newcastle, chancellor, 67

Perne, Dr Andrew, master of Peterhouse, vice-chancellor, 43, 63

Philpott, Dr Henry, master of St Catharine's College [vice-chancellor and bishop], 41

Plague, 13, 62-3, 63 n.

Plume, the Rev. Dr Thomas, benefactor, 75

Pope, bulls of, 2, 3 n., 19; Eugenius IV, 25; Honorius I, 25; Sergius I, 25

Praelectors' Lists, 12, 31

Press, University, 22-3, 28-9; accounts of, 35; archives of, 68-70

Preston, Dr Thomas, master of Trinity Hall, vice-chancellor, 11

Printer to the University, privileged person, 47; records of, 69-70; Thomas, Thomas, 70; Watts, Richard, 70; Whinn, Matthew, 13

Privileged Persons, 47, 50, 51, 57-9, 59 n.

Privy Council, 65, 67

Prize, Seatonian, 77

Proctors, 1, 5, 6, 7, 14, 16, 27, 34, 42-4, 52, 55-7, 60-1; records, accounts, 4, 6, 34-5; Books, 15, 27; indentures, 1, 5, 34, 43; Leet rolls, 11, 56, 56 n., 74; 'Registrum Librorum', etc., 4, 17 n.; 'Registra', 7, 28

Professorships: Hulsean, 75; Jacksonian, 40; Knightbridge, 76; Lady Margaret, 8, 40; Lowndean, 75; Lucasian, 41, 75; Norrisian, 77; Plumian, 41, 75; Regius, of Divinity, 76; Sadleirian, 76, 77; Woodwardian, 41. *See also* Appendix B

Queen, in Council, 67, 77

Raleigh, Sir Walter, 33

Rannoch, John Stewart of, benefactor, 77, 78

Rede Lectures, 17, 38

Regent House, *see* 'New Chapel'

Register, *see* Registrary; office, *see* Registry

Registers, 'Acta Curiae', 8, 11, 12, 73; matriculation, 8, 11, 30, 58-9; subscription, 12 n., 32-4, 73; wills, 7, 8, 51, 58, 73

Registrary, 6-14, 16-23, 45-7 *passim*, 67; clerk to courts, 50; creation of office of, 7, 28; custodian of records of 'Sex Viri', 52; duties and salary of, 10-14; records made by, 8, 12, 14, 46-7; records now in guard-books, 8 n., 12 n., 13 n., 21 n., 22 n.
    Caryl, Lynford, 20; Clark, John Willis, 22, 41; Hobbys, Robert, 7-8, 28; Hustler, William, 21; Luard, Henry Richards, 22, 23, 32 n., 68; Mere, John, 8, 9, 12, 17, 38-40, 46-7, 54, 54 n.; Romilly,

Registrary (*cont.*)
 Joseph, 22, 22 n., 66 n.; Smith, Thomas, 11; Stokys, Matthew, 9, 10, 12, 46-7, 57; Tabor, James, 10, 11, 12, 13, 18, 45, 46, 49, 63; Whinn, Matthew, 13, 46
Registry, 9, 10, 11, 18-23, 74
Richard II, 25, 48, 55
Romilly, Joseph, registrary, 22, 22 n., 66 n.
Rubens, Peter Paul, 33
Rustat, Tobias, 77; donation of, 40, 76, 77
Rysley, Master William, 4, 5, 6, 17

Sadleir, Lady, benefactor, 76, 77
Saint Bene't, church of, 9, 39
Saint Dionysius, feast of, 1
Saint Mary the Great, church of, 2, 4, 38, 40, 71
Scholarships:
 Battie, 78
 Craven, 78
 Stewart of Rannoch, 78
 see also Appendix B
Seaton, the Rev. Thomas, benefactor, 77
Senate, Council of, 23, 30, 32 n., 72
Senate House, 20, 71
Senate House Hill, 17
Sergius I, 25
Sewers, 63, 63 n.; Books of, 63; Clerk to Commissioners of, 10; Orders for, 63
'Sex Viri' [now 'Septemviri'], 52
Sherlock, Dr Thomas [master of St Catharine's College and bishop], vice-chancellor, 43
Smoult, the Rev. Dr Thomas, benefactor, 76
Soane, John, plans of, 21
Spinning House, 59-61, 61 n., 74
Statutes, 26, 27, 67, 72; 'Statuta Antiqua', 1, 1 n., 3 n., 6 n., 26, 72; Statutes of Elizabeth I, 15, 18, 27, 33, 45 nn., 50, 65, 72
Stokys, Matthew, bedell, registrary, 9, 10, 12, 46-7, 57; Alms Houses, 64; Book, 9 n., 38 n., 47, 47 n.
Storey's Charity, 64
Subscription, *see* Registers
Supplicats, for degrees, 12, 31

Tabor, James, registrary, 10, 11, 12, 13, 18, 45, 46, 49, 63
Taxors, 42-3, 50, 55, 57, 57 n.
Temple, Henry John, Viscount Palmerston, 61
Tey, Robert, 5
Thomas, Thomas, printer to the university, 70
Thornton, Dr Nigel de, 5, 39
Thorpe, Lady Grace, benefactor, 3

Thorpe, Sir William, benefactor, 3, 37
Trinity College, Dublin, 34

University Chest, *see* Chest, Common, of the university

Vestry, of 'New Chapel', 4, 14, 15, 19, 20
Vice-chancellor, 1, 4, 12, 14, 16, 19, 65; accounts of, 35, 73; jurisdiction of, in university courts, 49-52, 73; jurisdiction jointly held with officials of town, 62-3; licensing powers, 47, 56, 61, 74; office of, books and 'tradita' of, 43-4; mode of election to and tenure of, 42-3
 Ashton, Dr Charles, 43; Beale, Dr Jerome, 16; Butts, Dr Henry, 13, 62; Fisher, Dr John, 7; Jegon, Dr John, 11, 58 n.; Perne, Dr Andrew, 43, 63; Preston, Dr Thomas, 11; Sherlock, Dr Thomas, 43; Yonge [*alias* Young], Dr John, 56; *see also* Parker, Dr Matthew; Wren, Dr Matthew
Victoria, Queen, 66, 66 n.
Visitation proposed, of Archbishop Laud, 11, 18, 66
Visits, royal, 66, 66 n.
Votes, to elective offices, papers recording, 45-6
Vouchers to Accounts, 36, 47, 69

Wallis, Dr John, 20
Water supply, 53, 61-4
Watson, Simon, 56
Watts, Richard, printer to the university, 70
Webb, Dr William, master of Clare College [vice-chancellor], 41
Whinn, Matthew, registrary, printer to the university, 13, 46
Whitgift, Dr John [formerly master of Pembroke College and of Trinity College, and vice-chancellor], archbishop of Canterbury, 65
Winstanley, Denys Arthur, 27 n., 32, 33 nn., 51 n., 67 n.
Wiseham, Master Guy, 32, 33
Wolsey, Cardinal, 25, 34
Woodward, Dr John, benefactor, 77
Worts' Causeway, 64; Endowment, 64, 75
Wray's Charity, 64
Wren, Dr Matthew master of Peterhouse, vice-chancellor and bishop, 12 n., 13, 17, 18, 39

Yonge [*alias* Young], Dr John [master of Pembroke College], vice-chancellor, 56

Zouche, Dr Eudo [? Guy] de la, chancellor, 3

INDEX TO MUNIMENTS OF TITLE IN APPENDIX B

Ashwell, Herts., 76

Balsham, Cambs., 75
Barton, Cambs., 75
Binstead, Hants., 76
Bishopstoke, Hants., 76
Bishop Sutton (in Chew Magna), Som.,
   77
Brettenham, Suff., 78
Burwell, Cambs., 75

Chelmsford, Essex, 76
Chew Magna, Som., 77
Clive, Ches., 75
Cottenham, Cambs., 75

East Grinstead (manor of Cansern), Sussex,
   78
Elworth, Ches., 75

Hartfield (manor of Cansern), Sussex, 78
Hitcham, Suff., 78

Keynsham, Som., 78
Kilmeston, Hants., 76
Kislingbury, Northants., 77

Landbeach, Cambs., 75

London (Eastcheap), 77

Middlewich, Ches., 75

Neatham (in Binstead), Hants., 76

Over, Cambs., 75
Overton, Ches., 75
Ovington, Norf., 77

Pidley, Hunts., 76

Rampton, Cambs., 75
Raveningham, Norf., 77
Ridgewell, Essex, 76

Sandbach, Ches., 75
Smallwood, Ches., 75
Somersham, Hunts., 76
Spalding (manor of Fleet), Lincs., 77

Terrington, Norf., 77
Therfield, Herts., 76
Thurleigh, Beds., 75
Thurlton, Norf., 77

Writtle, Essex, 76

For EU product safety concerns, contact us at Calle de José Abascal, 56–1°, 28003 Madrid, Spain or eugpsr@cambridge.org.